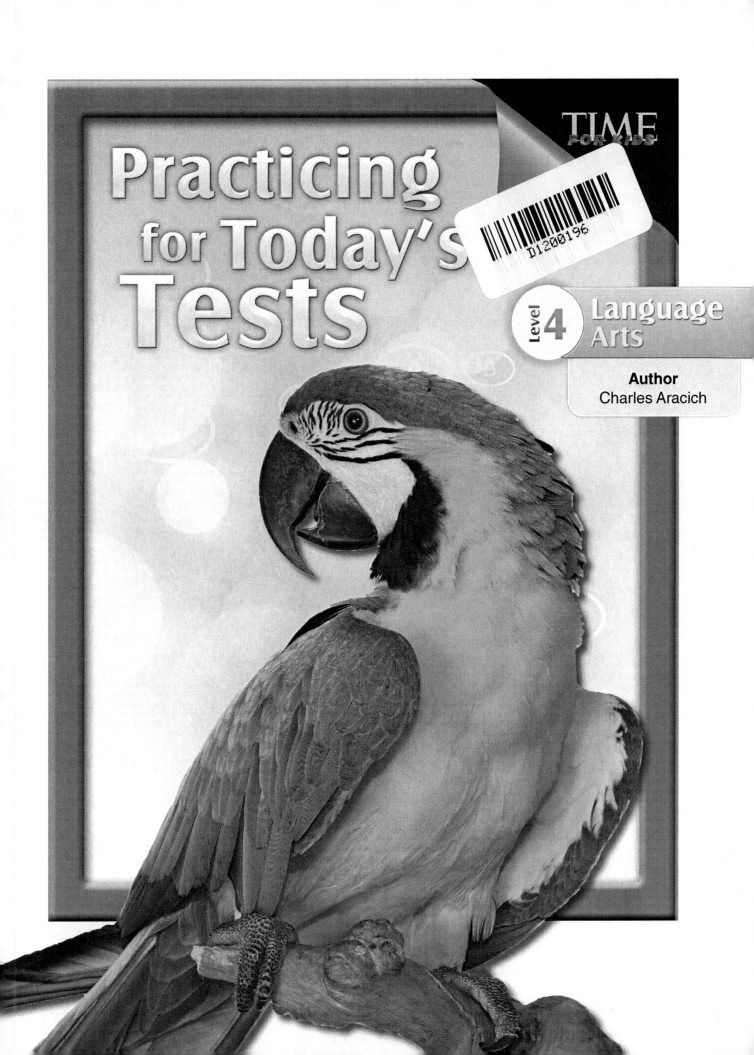

Practicing for Today's Tests

TIME FOR KIDS

Level 4 Language Arts

Author
Charles Aracich

Introduction Author

Delia E. Racines, Ph.D.
Faculty, University of Southern California
USC Language Academy

Publishing Credits

Corinne Burton, M.A.Ed., *President*;
Emily R. Smith, M.A.Ed., *Editorial Director*;
Debra J. Housel, M.S.Ed., *Editor*; Jennifer Wilson,
Editor; Courtney Patterson, *Multimedia Designer*;
Stephanie Bernard, *Assistant Editor*;
Monique Dominguez, *Production Artist*

Image Credits

p 66: iStock; All other images from Shutterstock unless noted otherwise

Standards

© Copyright 2010. National Governors Association Center for Best Practices and Council of Chief State School Officers. All rights reserved.

Shell Education

5301 Oceanus Drive
Huntington Beach, CA 92649-1030
http://www.shelleducation.com
ISBN 978-1-4258-1437-3
© 2015 Shell Educational Publishing, Inc.

The classroom teacher may reproduce copies of materials in this book for classroom use only. The reproduction of any part for an entire school or school system is strictly prohibited. No part of this publication may be transmitted, stored, or recorded in any form without written permission from the publisher.

Table of Contents

Today's Next Generation Tests

"To be college and career ready, students must now read across a broad range of high-quality texts from diverse cultures and times in history."

—Delia E. Racines, Ph.D.

Education is currently undergoing a dramatic shift when it comes to the ways we measure and assess for learning. Educational standards across the nation are designed to provide clear and meaningful goals for our students. These standards serve as a frame of reference for educators, parents, and students and are most critical when decisions must be made about curriculum, textbooks, assessments, and other aspects of instructional programs (Conley 2014). Part of the disconnect with standards in the recent past has been the vast differences and lack of consistency in expectations that became a major concern for the quality of education students were receiving across the country (Conley 2014; Wiley and Wright 2004).

Standards in education in the United States are not a new concept. However, the role of educational standards has recently shifted to not only ensure that all students have access to equitable education no matter where they live, but also to ensure a more consistent national expectation for what all students should know to be successful in a rapidly changing economy and society (Kornhaber, Griffith, and Tyler 2014).

Scales, scores, and assessments are absolutely necessary to ascertain the current status of students. This kind of data is vital for teachers to understand what is missing and what the next steps should be. The real question about assessment isn't whether we should assess but rather what kinds of assessments should be used. Along with the current shift to more consistent and rigorous standards, states now measure student progress with assessments that require higher-order thinking skills necessary for preparation for college and/or careers.

So, what is this new yardstick that is being used? How is it better than yardsticks of the past? And how do we best prepare students to be measured with this yardstick in a way that tells the whole story? The next generation tests intend to provide results that are comparable across all states and will use more performance-based tasks as well as technology-enhanced items. This is very different in comparison to the standardized testing that teachers, students, and parents are used to (National Governors Association Center for Best Practices 2010; Rothman 2013).

The following descriptions serve as explanations of how the three most prominent next-generation tests are different from assessments of the past.

Today's Next Generation Tests *(cont.)*

Partnership for Assessment of Readiness for College and Careers (PARCC)

The PARCC assessment is a common set of computer-based, K–12 assessments in English language arts and mathematics. These assessments replace previous state tests in grades 3–11 used to meet the requirements of the Elementary and Secondary Education Act (PARCC 2013). The most significant difference in the PARCC tests is the use of performance tasks that ask students to apply their knowledge to solve extended problems rather than simply regurgitate answers (Rothman 2013).

PARCC consists of four assessments a year. The two optional assessments include diagnostic assessments (in reading, writing, and mathematics) that may be administered at the beginning of each school year and as mid-year assessments to help predict students' likely end-of-year performances.

The two required summative assessments consist of a performance task and an end-of-year test for each grade. Previously, in English language arts, many states did not assess writing and few assessed critical-thinking skills. The PARCC assessment does both. The performance-based assessment is in English language arts and mathematics and includes asking students to analyze literature as well as narrative writing tasks. Students also take the end-of-year assessments in English language arts and mathematics. The results of the two tests are combined to determine the summative assessment score (PARCC 2013). Lastly, a separate speaking and listening component is required and can be administered anytime during the academic year. The results of the speaking and listening component are not be combined with the other assessments to determine students' summative assessment scores.

Many of today's standardized tests are administered online.

Today's Next Generation Tests (cont.)

Smarter Balanced Assessment Consortium (SBAC)

The SBAC is also developing summative assessments in English language arts and mathematics. Their assessments have two major components: performance tasks and an end-of-the-year computer adaptive test. Computer adaptive tests mean that questions are adjusted based on students' previous responses. These two major components are administered during the last 12 weeks of the school year (SBAC 2014). The computer adaptive test feature, which is the biggest difference from the PARCC, is intended to enable administrators and teachers to use results within weeks to more efficiently and quickly identify students' ability levels in an effort to differentiate instruction. The SBAC assessments go beyond multiple-choice tests to include short constructed responses, extended constructed responses, and performance tasks. These allow students to complete in-depth projects that demonstrate both analytical skills and real-world problem solving (SBAC 2014). Performance tasks are online in reading, writing, and mathematics and may also be administered as part of the optional interim assessments throughout the year. Results will be available within weeks after a student completes a performance task.

State of Texas Assessment of Academic Readiness (STAAR®)

The STAAR® replaced the Texas Assessment of Knowledge and Skills (TAKS). It was developed and adopted by the Texas School Board of Education within the Texas Education Agency. This assessment focuses on readiness for college and/or careers with test questions that focus on rigor and critical analysis.

For elementary school and middle school, the tests cover the same subjects and grades as the previous state testing program, the TAKS. The most significant differences between the TAKS and the STAAR® are apparent at the high school level with 12 end-of-course assessments that focus on fewer skills in a deeper manner and replace previous grade-specific tests (Texas Education Agency 2014). The STAAR® assesses the Texas Essential Knowledge and Skills. However, there are a greater number of items with higher cognitive demands. In writing, students are required to write two essays instead of one.

Categories of Questions

In order for students today to be better prepared for college and/or careers, they must be able to read widely and deeply across a range of informational and literary texts (National Governors Association Center for Best Practices 2010). In today's standards, there are often three categories of reading standards. On assessments, these categories are represented by three categories of questions. The questions include new terminology that defines specific skills and understandings that all students must demonstrate. **Note:** See *Appendix B* (pages 100–103) for how these categories are represented in each practice exercise in this book.

Overall, today's college and career readiness reading standards depict the picture of what students should be able to exhibit with increasing proficiency and on a regular basis. To be college and career ready, students must now read across a broad range of high-quality texts from diverse cultures and times in history. The reading standards emphasize the skills necessary to critically read and continuously make connections among ideas and texts. Students also learn to distinguish poor reasoning as well as ambiguities in texts. The following explanation of the terms related to each of the three reading categories will better prepare educators and parents for today's tests.

Key Ideas and Details

This category stresses the importance of understanding specific information in various texts. Overall, students must be able to identify specific details and then gain deeper meaning from what is read. Specifically, this category requires students to be able to do the following things.

Students should be able to . . .	To show how they know this, students must . . .
read text closely to really understand what it says.	identify specific details from the text.
make conclusions based on what they identify from a text.	say or write specific details to support their conclusions.
determine the main idea or theme from a text and analyze its development.	identify and summarize key supporting details that support the theme or main idea.
figure out how and why individuals, events, or ideas develop and interact over the course of a text.	explain details about how characters and/ or the story develop at different times throughout the text from the beginning to the end.

Categories of Questions *(cont.)*

Craft and Structure

This category stresses the importance of being able to identify patterns of various text structures to more easily synthesize and summarize information. Physical text structures (captions, pictures, diagrams, italicized print, bold print, etc.) are purposely used in texts to organize different types of information. This is true for both fiction and nonfiction texts. Specifically, this category requires students to be able to do the following things.

Students should be able to . . .	To show how they know this, students must . . .
interpret words and phrases as they are used in technical, connotative, or figurative texts.	explain the purposes of different types of texts and distinguish what kinds of words or phrases are used in each type.
analyze how specific word choices shape meaning or tone.	identify and explain why certain words are used and how different words alter the feelings readers experience from texts.
analyze the parts or structures of a text.	identify the names and purposes of each different structure within a text.
explain the relationships between parts or structures within a text.	explain how sentences, paragraphs, and larger portions of texts relate to one another and the whole text.
figure out how point of view shapes the content and style of a text.	explain how different perspectives could change the meaning of a text.
figure out how purpose changes the content and style of a text.	explain how different purposes could alter the meaning of a text.

© Shell Education

Categories of Questions *(cont.)*

Integration of Knowledge and Ideas

This category stresses the importance of being able to understand the main idea of texts and analyze details presented in various formats. Students should then be able to draw conclusions based on the text, interpret the purpose and structure of texts, and apply the meaning across other texts and knowledge. In general, students should compare and contrast texts and ultimately increase comprehensibility of more complex texts. Specifically, this category requires students to be able to do the following things.

Students should be able to . . .	To show how they know this, students must . . .
evaluate content presented in various formats (e.g., in writing, visually, via media, and numerically).	describe what they understand about the content through various formats.
integrate or put together cross-curricular content that is presented in different formats.	explain how ideas presented in various formats are related to one another.
outline what the argument is in a text.	identify specific claims in a text that include how valid the reasoning is in the argument, how relevant the reasoning is to the argument, and whether there is enough evidence to support the argument.
analyze how two or more texts address similar themes or topics to build knowledge or to compare the approaches the authors take.	identify themes of multiple texts and then describe similarities and differences between the texts.
compare the approaches different authors take.	identify the approaches different authors take and then describe similarities and differences between them.

Making It Meaningful

The section has been included to make this book's test practice more meaningful. The purpose of this section is to provide sample guiding questions framed around a specific practice exercise. This will serve as a meaningful and real-life application of the test practice. Each of the guiding questions serves as a thinking prompt to ensure that the three categories of the reading standards have been considered. The guiding questions may be used with students as a teacher-led think aloud or to individually assess how students are approaching and understanding complex texts. The framework used in this model serves as a template for how to approach other fiction and nonfiction texts. The template supports educators in preparing students for today's tests and helps make meaning of the reading standards to ultimately ensure that the learning becomes more meaningful for all students.

Begin with the Craft and Structure reading standards in mind by asking students these questions:

What type of text is this?

What is the purpose of this type of text?

Identify what text structures are used in this text and why.

What is the relationship among certain vocabulary words?

How do the words shape the tone?

Then, with the Key Ideas and Details reading standards in mind, coach students to do the following:

Underline the key details you have noticed so far.

Write a summary sentence with these details as support.

List or create a timeline of important events in the character's story.

Finally, check for understanding with the Integration of Knowledge and Ideas reading standards in mind by asking students to do the following:

Make connections across other content areas.

Explain how varied ideas relate to one another.

Making It Meaningful *(cont.)*

When questions refer to specific sentences, guide the students in the following way:

"This question references a specific sentence in the text. Go back and **highlight** or <u>underline</u> this sentence. Then, reread the text around that sentence to find the answer the question."

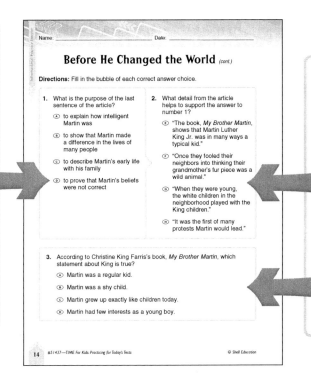

For all questions, students should do the following:

"Ask yourself what the directions are asking you to do Do you need to analyze, infer, evaluate, formulate, describe, support, explain, summarize, compare, contrast, predict, fill in, complete, etc.?"

When students are asked vocabulary questions, help them in the following way:

"Find the specific vocabulary word in the text and circle it. Use the other words around it to figure out its meaning using context clues."

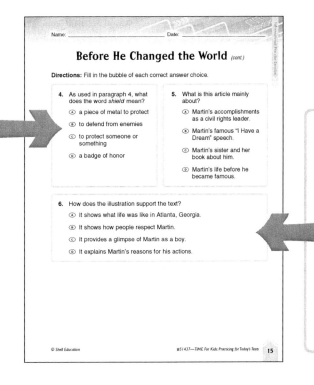

Sometimes, students will be asked questions about graphics or captions.

"Illustrations, pictures, graphics, and captions are types of text structures. What is the purpose of the specific text structure in this text?"

Making It Meaningful (cont.)

When students have to use the text to defend their answers, guide them in the following way:

"Find the specific quoted statement in the text. Underline other specific details that support this statement and your response to the prompt."

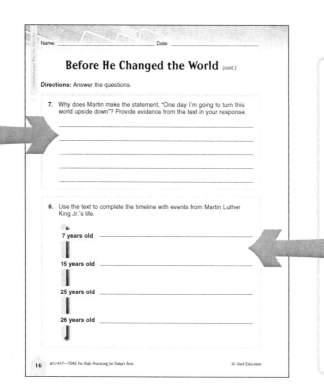

If students need to complete graphic organizers, use guiding questions to help them determine how the text can help them respond.

"What is the purpose of a timeline? Find and write details about the character's life to complete the timeline."

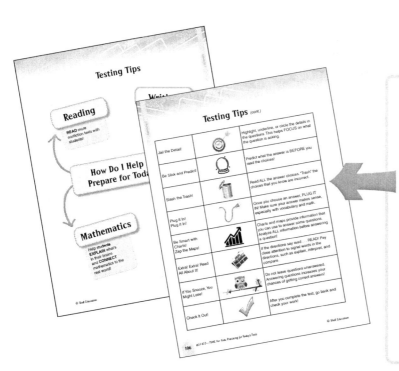

To support students in preparing for today's tests, send home the Testing Tips flyers on pages 105–106. There is one page intended to guide parents in how to prepare their children and a second page to help students understand ways they can be more succcssful while taking tests.

Name: _____   Date: _____

Before He Changed the World

Directions: Read this text and respond to the questions on pages 14–16.

1   You know Martin Luther King Jr. as the leader of the Civil Rights Movement in the United States. You may have heard part of his famous "I Have a Dream" speech. But before Martin Luther King Jr. was a great leader, he was a little boy. He played games and played jokes on people.

2   This picture of King's childhood is in a book. It was written by his big sister, Christine King Farris. The book, *My Brother Martin*, shows that Martin Luther King Jr. was in many ways a typical kid.

3   Christine and Martin had a little brother named Alfred. They grew up in Atlanta, Georgia. Their father, Martin Luther King Sr., was a minister. Their mother, Alberta, was a musician. The kids liked to play board games and checkers. They also liked to play pranks. Once they fooled their neighbors into thinking their grandmother's fur piece was a wild animal.

Chris Soentpiet, from *My Brother Martin*, By Christine King Farris, Simon & Schuster

A Segregated South

4   There was lots of love in the King home. But the world outside was often cruel. Their parents tried to shield the children from the unfair laws that kept black and white people apart. The Kings hardly ever took the kids to the movies. They didn't like how African Americans had to use a separate entrance to the theater. They could only sit in the balcony.

5   When they were young, the white children in the neighborhood played with the King children. Then one day, when Martin was 7, the white kids said they could no longer play together. Martin told his mother, "One day I'm going to turn this world upside down!"

6   Martin was very smart. He skipped grades 3 and 12. He went to college when he was just 15. By the time he was 25, he was a pastor of a church in Montgomery, Alabama. A year later he became a leader of the Montgomery Bus Boycott in 1955. African Americans in Montgomery refused to ride the buses as long as they had to sit in the back. It was the first of many protests Martin would lead. Before he was done, he did turn the world upside down.

Name: _____   Date: _____

Before He Changed the World *(cont.)*

Directions: Fill in the bubble of each correct answer choice.

1. What is the purpose of the last sentence of the article?

    Ⓐ to explain how intelligent Martin was

    Ⓑ to show that Martin made a difference in the lives of many people

    Ⓒ to describe Martin's early life with his family

    Ⓓ to prove that Martin's beliefs were not correct

2. What detail from the article helps to support the answer to number 1?

    Ⓔ "The book, *My Brother Martin*, shows that Martin Luther King Jr. was in many ways a typical kid."

    Ⓕ "Once they fooled their neighbors into thinking their grandmother's fur piece was a wild animal."

    Ⓖ "When they were young, the white children in the neighborhood played with the King children."

    Ⓗ "It was the first of many protests Martin would lead."

3. According to Christine King Farris's book, *My Brother Martin*, which statement about King is true?

    Ⓐ Martin was a regular kid.

    Ⓑ Martin was a shy child.

    Ⓒ Martin grew up exactly like children today.

    Ⓓ Martin had few interests as a young boy.

Name: _____   Date: _____

Before He Changed the World *(cont.)*

Directions: Fill in the bubble of each correct answer choice.

---

4. As used in paragraph 4, what does the word *shield* mean?

Ⓐ a piece of metal to protect

Ⓑ to defend from enemies

Ⓒ to protect someone or something

Ⓓ a badge of honor

---

5. What is this article mainly about?

Ⓐ Martin's accomplishments as a civil rights leader.

Ⓑ Martin's famous "I Have a Dream" speech.

Ⓒ Martin's sister and her book about him.

Ⓓ Martin's life before he became famous.

---

6. How does the illustration support the text?

Ⓐ It shows what life was like in Atlanta, Georgia.

Ⓑ It shows how people respect Martin.

Ⓒ It provides a glimpse of Martin as a boy.

Ⓓ It explains Martin's reasons for his actions.

Name: _____ Date: _____

Before He Changed the World *(cont.)*

Directions: Answer the questions.

7. Why does Martin make the statement, "One day I'm going to turn this world upside down"? Provide evidence from the text in your response.

_____

_____

_____

_____

8. Use the text to complete the timeline with events from Martin Luther King Jr.'s life.

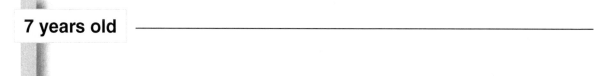

7 years old _____

15 years old _____

25 years old _____

26 years old _____

     © Shell Education

Name: _____   Date: _____

Little Bugs, Big Stink

Directions: Read this text and respond to the questions on pages 18–20.

1   The brown marmorated stinkbug deserves its name. When squashed or bothered, this bug gives off a strong odor. It smells like a skunk! Stinkbugs first appeared in the United States about 15 years ago. Now the insect has spread to at least 40 states. Experts say the stinkbug population is still growing.

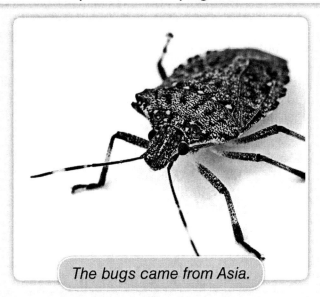

The bugs came from Asia.

2   Scientists aren't sure why stinkbugs are spreading. Mike Raupp is an entomologist. He is a scientist who studies insects. He works at the University of Maryland. He says there was an especially high number of stinkbugs in 2013. "Nobody really knows why there were so many that year," he told TIME For Kids.

3   Stinkbugs don't like the cold. When fall brings cooler weather, they seek warmth. Then the bugs invade people's homes. Fortunately, the insects don't sting, bite, or carry diseases. But when stepped on or sucked into a vacuum cleaner, they give off a bad smell.

4   Stinkbugs cause trouble in the environment. They eat fruit and vegetable crops. They have caused millions of dollars in crop losses for American farmers. The United States government is looking for ways to get rid of them. One idea is to make a chemical that attracts the stinkbugs. The chemical would be put into traps. The insects would enter the traps and not be able to get out.

5   Another idea is to use the stinkbug's natural enemies. Scientists are studying a wasp from Asia. They think it might help to control stinkbugs. American farmers hope scientists solve this stinky problem soon!

Name: _____   Date: _____

Little Bugs, Big Stink *(cont.)*

Directions: Fill in the bubble of each correct answer choice.

1. Which word in the second paragraph can be a synonym for *entomologist*?

    Ⓐ insect

    Ⓑ number

    Ⓒ year

    Ⓓ scientist

2. Based on the clues in the text, what month of the year would you be most likely to find a stinkbug in your house?

    Ⓐ April

    Ⓑ June

    Ⓒ August

    Ⓓ October

3. Why does the author use the word *invade* when describing stinkbugs in the home?

    Ⓐ The stinkbugs are like aliens from another planet.

    Ⓑ The stinkbugs are unwelcome guests.

    Ⓒ The stinkbugs eat food from people's homes.

    Ⓓ The stinkbugs threaten humans' health.

Name: _____ Date: _____

Lighting the Way

Directions: Read this text and respond to the questions on pages 22–24.

1   Ann Makosinski is a smart young woman—and she has an award to prove it! The teenager from British Columbia, Canada, invented a flashlight that works without batteries. Ann entered her invention in the 2013 Google Science Fair. It won the top prize for her age group. "This experience was life-changing," Ann told TIME For Kids. "I feel so inspired."

A Simple Solution

2   Inventors often create things to solve problems. That's the case with Ann. Her bright idea was sparked by a desire to help friends living in the Philippines. Their families could not afford electricity. This meant that they had no lights to study by at night. The kids had trouble doing their homework. Ann wanted to solve this dilemma. "People radiate so much energy," Ann says. "Why not capture and use some of it?"

3   Here's how her invention works. The flashlight has a hollow aluminum tube in its center. The flashlight's handle has tiles on it. The tiles draw heat from your hand and also from the surrounding air. The heat makes energy. It powers the flashlight's bulbs.

4   There is still work to be done on these "hollow flashlights." Ann would like them to become available to people who live in poor countries. She also wants to put the finishing touches on her flashlight's design.

5   What's next for Ann? The busy teen is working on another project. It is hands-free headlamps for kids. "So many people face problems with something we take for granted," Ann says. "I want to provide a solution."

Ann explains her invention at the Google Science Fair.

Andrew Federman

Name: _____ Date: _____

Lighting the Way (cont.)

Directions: Fill in the bubble of each correct answer choice.

1. What is Ann's reason for creating her flashlight?

   Ⓐ She is interested in winning a science fair.

   Ⓑ She knows that her invention could make her a lot of money.

   Ⓒ She wants to help people in places that lack electricity.

   Ⓓ She wants to solve a problem she has while reading at night.

2. Which two questions might the man in the photograph ask Ann?

   Ⓐ What inspired this idea?

   Ⓑ Where do the batteries go in your flashlight?

   Ⓒ Can you tell me about the feet lamps you are working on?

   Ⓓ How does it feel to compete in the science fair?

3. Which sentence from the article helps the reader to understand the meaning of the word *radiate*?

   Ⓐ "The flashlight's handle has tiles on it."

   Ⓑ "The tiles draw heat from your hand and also from the surrounding air."

   Ⓒ "The heat makes energy."

   Ⓓ "It powers the flashlight's bulbs."

© Shell Education

Lighting the Way *(cont.)*

Directions: Fill in the bubble of each correct answer choice.

4. Read these sentences from paragraph 1: "'This experience was life-changing,' Ann told TIME For Kids. 'I feel so inspired.'" These sentences help predict why Ann might . . .

   Ⓐ be satisfied with winning the contest.

   Ⓑ want to take some time off from working.

   Ⓒ show off her award to her classmates.

   Ⓓ continue creating inventions.

5. Which details support Ann's statements from number 4? There is more than one correct choice.

   Ⓔ She wants to finish the flashlight's design.

   Ⓕ She is a very intelligent girl.

   Ⓖ She hopes her flashlight will help people in poor countries.

   Ⓗ She is working on a hands-free headlamp for kids.

6. This article is mainly about a young woman who . . .

   Ⓐ hopes to win top prize at the Google Science Fair.

   Ⓑ wants to create as many inventions as possible.

   Ⓒ creates a solution to a problem in another part of the world.

   Ⓓ explains how her flashlight operates without batteries.

Name: _____ Date: _____

Lighting the Way (cont.)

Directions: Answer the questions.

7. Number the events from the passage in order.

   _____ Ann enters the flashlight in the 2013 Google Science Fair.

   _____ Poor families do not have enough money to pay for electricity.

   _____ Ann decides to create a flashlight that does not need batteries.

   _____ Students have a difficult time completing their homework.

8. At the end of the article, Ann says, "So many people face problems with something we take for granted. I want to provide a solution." Explain what you think she means by this statement.

   _____

   _____

   _____

   _____

   _____

   _____

   _____

   _____

   _____

Hoop Dreams

Directions: Read this text and respond to the questions on pages 26–28.

1   Dancer R.J. Lopez carries on an American Indian tradition. R.J. loves to perform. The first grader from Arizona is a hoop dancer. He won first place for his age group at the 2013 World Championship Hoop Dance Contest, in Phoenix, Arizona. "My favorite part is showing everybody my cool moves," he told TIME For Kids. But R.J. doesn't dance just to show off. He enjoys taking part in an important American Indian tradition.

What Is Hoop Dancing?

2   Hoop dancing is a big part of some American Indian cultures. People move to the sound of drums and chants. They use the hoops to make designs and shapes that tell stories.

3   R.J.'s winning dance began with five hoops. He picked up more hoops, one at a time. He spun them with his arms and jumped through the hoops. He put the hoops together to make shapes.

4   By the end of the dance, R.J. had four hoops on each arm and five hoops on his legs and around his body. People clapped when he held hoops together to look like an eagle's wings. "Keeping all of them on at the same time is hard," R.J. said.

5   Some people take classes to learn how to dance. Not R.J. He learned by copying his uncles. "We dance as a family," says R.J.'s mom, Christy. "We do it for fun."

6   R.J.'s dad, Rito, says dance has a serious side, too. "We always teach our children that when they dance, they dance for the elders and for those who are no longer able to dance, to give them strength and joy," he says. R.J. is doing his part to keep the tradition alive.

R.J. Lopez dances at a festival in Arizona. He makes shapes with the hoops.

Apphia Shirley—Heard Museum

Hoop Dreams (cont.)

Directions: Fill in the bubble of each correct answer choice.

1. Why does R.J. Lopez perform his dance?

   Ⓐ to show off in front of others

   Ⓑ to win contests and money

   Ⓒ to keep a tradition going

   Ⓓ to set world records

2. The photograph and caption best support what idea from the selection?

   Ⓐ R.J. is practicing to perform in front of others.

   Ⓑ R.J. is putting on a show for an audience.

   Ⓒ R.J. is about to set a world record for his dance.

   Ⓓ R.J. is getting ready to begin his dance for an audience.

3. Read this sentence from paragraph 1: "My favorite part is showing everybody my cool moves." What does this tell us about R.J.?

   Ⓐ He is strong.

   Ⓑ He is responsible.

   Ⓒ He is selfish.

   Ⓓ He is confident.

Name: _____   Date: _____

Hoop Dreams *(cont.)*

Directions: Fill in the bubble of each correct answer choice.

4. What sentence from the text suggests that R.J. is very talented?

   Ⓐ "Some people take classes to learn how to dance."

   Ⓑ "R.J.'s dad, Rito, says dance has a serious side, too."

   Ⓒ "He enjoys taking part in an important American Indian tradition."

   Ⓓ "People clapped when he held hoops together to look like an eagle's wings."

5. Based on clues from the article, which example would best display R.J.'s hoop talents?

   Ⓔ spinning two hoops on his arm

   Ⓕ keeping a hoop in the air for five seconds

   Ⓖ telling a story about turtles using hoops

   Ⓗ rotating a hoop around his neck while chanting

6. Why did the author include the last paragraph in the article?

   Ⓐ to show that the traditions of the family are important

   Ⓑ to explain how hard R.J. works to improve

   Ⓒ to prove to the reader that hoop dancing is exciting

   Ⓓ to encourage others to perform hoop dancing

Name: _____   Date: _____

Hoop Dreams *(cont.)*

Directions: Answer the questions.

7. How does R.J. perform his winning dance? Include at least four details from the text in the chart below.

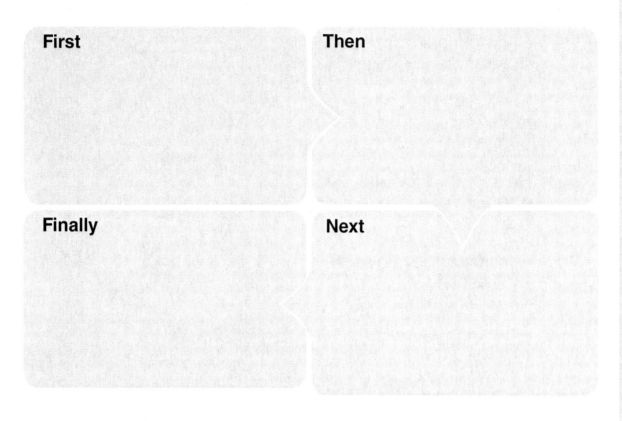

First

Then

Finally

Next

8. What detail do you learn about R.J. from reading the fifth paragraph?

_____

_____

_____

_____

Name: _____   Date: _____

They're Back!

Directions: Read this text and respond to the questions on pages 30–32.

1   Each year, about 10,000 to 100,000 animal species die out. Many species have become extinct during Earth's history. Extinction means an animal is gone forever.

2   At least it used to mean that. Scientists may now be able to bring back extinct species. Now, don't get excited. It doesn't mean the plot of the movie *Jurassic Park* is going to come true. Researchers need DNA to bring back a species. DNA is the chemical that carries the structure for every living thing. Dinosaurs have been gone for too long. None of their DNA remains in fossils.

3   But there's a real chance that we'll be able to bring back more recent species. This could include Ice Age animals like the woolly mammoth. In 2003, a team of Spanish and French scientists re-created the Pyrenean ibex. The new animal didn't survive long. But advances may change that.

4   If we can bring species back from the dead, should we? There may be benefits. Still, there's no way to know how it will turn out. For example, say we re-created passenger pigeons. Would they fit into their old habitats? Or might they crowd out existing species? And will people work less hard to protect animals if they know that scientists can reverse our mistakes?

5   Humans have caused many animal extinctions. Some people think we should correct our mistakes. Stewart Brand is a businessman and environmentalist. He says, "Humans have made a huge hole in nature. We have the ability now . . . to repair some of that damage."

6   But we should remember the lesson of *Jurassic Park*: Proceed with caution. And maybe leave the velociraptors alone!

Making a Comeback

The **GASTRIC BROODING FROG** was native to Australia until the 1980s.

The **PASSENGER PIGEON** numbered in the billions. It went extinct in 1914.

The **THYLACINE** is known as the Tasmanian tiger. It went extinct in the 1930s.

The **PYRENEAN IBEX** lived in Spain and Portugal. It went extinct in 2000.

Long Now Foundation; Cloning and Stem Cells

They're Back! *(cont.)*

Directions: Fill in the bubble of each correct answer choice.

1. Use the text in paragraph 2 to determine which animal has no chance of ever coming back from extinction.

    Ⓐ a woolly mammoth

    Ⓑ a Tyrannosaurus rex

    Ⓒ a passenger pigeon

    Ⓓ a Pyrenean ibex

2. Read this text from paragraph 5: "Humans have caused many animal extinctions. Some people think we should correct our mistakes. Stewart Brand is a businessman and environmentalist. He says, 'Humans have made a huge hole in nature. We have the ability now . . . to repair some of that damage.'" What does the phrase "a huge hole in nature" refer to?

    Ⓐ animals that have left and gone to other areas

    Ⓑ large openings in the ground all around the world

    Ⓒ living things that have been eliminated from the planet

    Ⓓ plants and animals from the Ice Age

3. What other event might cause a huge hole in nature?

    Ⓔ clearing a forest to build a new town

    Ⓕ monitoring animals in the wild

    Ⓖ opening more animal hospitals

    Ⓗ taking care of animals in zoos

© Shell Education

Name: _____   Date: _____

They're Back! (cont.)

Directions: Fill in the bubble of each correct answer choice.

4. Why does the author choose to show animals' pictures in the sidebar?

   Ⓐ Readers voted for the animals in a survey.

   Ⓑ They are interesting animals to look at.

   Ⓒ Scientists are considering bringing them back.

   Ⓓ These animals have already been brought back from extinction.

5. Which detail from the text gives the reader an idea of how close scientists are to accomplishing their goal?

   Ⓐ "In 2003, a team of Spanish and French scientists re-created the Pyrenean ibex."

   Ⓑ "Each year, about 10,000 to 100,000 animal species die out."

   Ⓒ "There may be benefits. Still, there's no way to know how it will turn out."

   Ⓓ "And maybe leave the velociraptors alone."

6. What is the main idea in paragraph 5?

   Ⓐ People should leave extinct animals alone.

   Ⓑ People are responsible for the extinction of many animals.

   Ⓒ There are similarities between the extinct animals and *Jurassic Park*.

   Ⓓ Stewart Brand has offered an interesting way to solve the problem of extinction.

Name: _____   Date: _____

They're Back! (cont.)

Directions: Answer the questions.

7. Underline two details in the text that show how re-creating an animal species might cause negative consequences.

8. Write two details from the text to support the newspaper headline.

JURASSIC PARK DINOSAURS:
GONE FOREVER

- _____

  _____

  _____

- _____

  _____

  _____

The Iditarod Is the Best Sport in the World *(cont.)*

3   What about marathon runners? It's true that marathon runners have many of the fine qualities of sled dogs, minus the bushy tails. But marathoners run a measly 26.2 miles (42.2 km). The Iditarod is 1,100 miles (1,770 km) long! A little bit of math will show you that sled dogs run 42.3 times farther than marathon runners.

4   It takes about 10 days for the sleds to go from Anchorage, Alaska, to the finish line in Nome, Alaska. Yes, some baseball games may feel like they're 10 days long, but that doesn't count. The Iditarod also has tradition. The race follows the 1925 route of a dog team. It brought life-saving medicine to sick kids in Nome. No other sport can say that.

Ice, Snow, and No Biting

5   The Iditarod is a team sport. The dogs must work together and not bite each other. It takes place in blizzards on icy trails. Hockey is played on ice, but it's indoors! How wimpy is that? Even the Iditarod spectators are tough. They watch the races in blizzards.

6   So forget about baseball and football. Leave behind marathons, soccer, and ice hockey. Go check out some real athletes and a real sport. Take a trip to Alaska and see the Iditarod!

These sled dogs run the race with determination.

Name: _____   Date: _____

The Iditarod Is the Best Sport in the World *(cont.)*

Directions: Fill in the bubble of each correct answer choice.

1. What is the author's purpose for writing this article?

   Ⓐ to explain how the Iditarod works

   Ⓑ to argue that football and baseball are not real sports

   Ⓒ to persuade the reader to try dogsledding

   Ⓓ to convince the reader that the Iditarod dog-sled race is the greatest sport

2. Which two details from the article support the answer to number 1?

   Ⓔ ". . . sled dogs run 42.3 times farther than marathon runners."

   Ⓕ "For example, football is exciting when there's a touchdown."

   Ⓖ "Go check out some real athletes and a real sport."

   Ⓗ "Most sled dogs are of a breed called 'husky.'"

3. What two conclusions can the reader draw from the caption on page 38?

   Ⓐ The race is very long.

   Ⓑ Sled dogs are amazing athletes.

   Ⓒ The weather is extremely cold.

   Ⓓ The Iditarod takes place once a year.

     © *Shell Education*

The Iditarod Is the Best Sport in the World *(cont.)*

Directions: Fill in the bubble of each correct answer choice.

4. Read this statement from paragraph 4: "The Iditarod also has tradition." Which detail from the text supports this statement?

   Ⓐ "It takes about 10 days for the sleds to go from Anchorage, Alaska, to the finish line in Nome, Alaska."

   Ⓑ "The Iditarod is 1,100 miles (1,770 km) long!"

   Ⓒ "The race follows the 1925 route of a dog team."

   Ⓓ "Even the Iditarod spectators are tough."

5. According to the article, how do the bushy tails help the dogs?

   Ⓐ They keep the dogs warm.

   Ⓑ They make the dogs run faster.

   Ⓒ They make the dogs better athletes.

   Ⓓ They keep the dogs focused.

6. Which detail supports the argument that the Iditarod is a team sport?

   Ⓐ The race is often run in a blizzard.

   Ⓑ The dogs have endurance and determination.

   Ⓒ The race starts in Anchorage and ends in Nome.

   Ⓓ The dogs must work together and not bite each other.

Name: _____ Date: _____

The Iditarod Is the Best
Sport in the World (cont.)

Directions: Answer the questions.

7. The article mentions other sports besides dog sledding. Label each box with one of these sports. Then, within each box, write the author's reason for why it is not as spectacular as dog sledding.

8. What is the main idea of this text? Support your answer with two details from the text.

    Main Idea _____

    _____

    • _____

    • _____

Name: _____ Date: _____

Anansi's Sons (cont.)

Directions: Fill in the bubble of each correct answer choice.

1. How does the illustration enhance the story?

   Ⓐ It helps the reader to picture Anansi's sons.

   Ⓑ It helps the reader who does not know what spiders are.

   Ⓒ It shows the reader the size of the fish.

   Ⓓ It helps the reader to visualize the danger that Anansi is in.

2. How does the introduction contribute to the story?

   Ⓐ It provides background information about Anansi.

   Ⓑ It introduces all the characters and the setting.

   Ⓒ It gives the reader a short history of Ghana.

   Ⓓ It explains why the author chose to write about Anansi.

3. Which detail applies to Anansi's sons? There is more than one correct choice.

   Ⓐ They all have unique talents.

   Ⓑ They act selfishly when they are all together.

   Ⓒ They are tired of having to save their father.

   Ⓓ They have names that tell what they can do.

Anansi's Sons (cont.)

Directions: Fill in the bubble of each correct answer choice.

4. Which sentence describes the end of the second problem for Anansi?

   Ⓐ "On clear nights, you can still see it."

   Ⓑ "He fell but fortunately Cushion waited on the ground to give his father a soft, safe landing."

   Ⓒ "From within the fish's belly, they could hear Anansi screaming."

   Ⓓ "One day, Anansi the spider went for a walk through the forest."

5. Which sentence lets the reader know that all the conflict has been resolved?

   Ⓔ "Stone Thrower grabbed a rock and threw it at the bird."

   Ⓕ "Anansi couldn't decide which son should receive the prize."

   Ⓖ "'I will give this gift to the son who saved me,' he announced."

   Ⓗ "Finally, Anansi was free from danger."

6. What is the gift that Anansi gives to Nyame?

   Ⓐ a star

   Ⓑ a cloud

   Ⓒ the moon

   Ⓓ the sun

© Shell Education

Name: _____ Date: _____

Anansi's Sons (cont.)

Directions: Answer the questions.

7. Use details from the story to name each of Anansi's sons and tell how each one helps his father.

_____

_____

_____

_____

_____

_____

8. Choose one son and use the web to describe why that son is the most helpful. Defend your choice with evidence from the story.

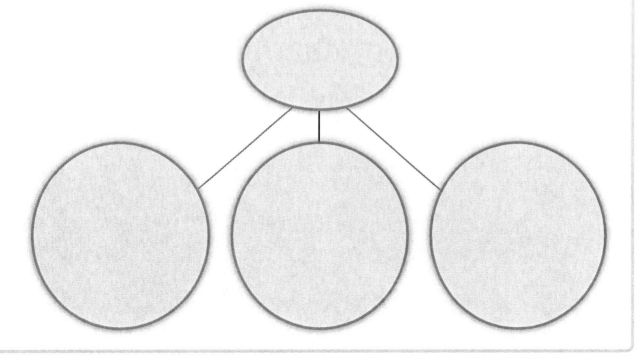

Name: _____   Date: _____

Bread and Roses

Directions: Read this story and respond to the questions on pages 54–56.

In 1912, thousands of textile (fabric making) workers in Lawrence, Massachusetts, went on strike to demand better wages and working conditions. Their slogan was "bread and roses." Many of the workers were children.

1   "Jedrek, watch out!"

2   Jedrek looked up as a cart loaded with thread careened toward him. As he jumped out of the way, he tripped and sprawled headfirst onto the factory floor. The heavy cart rolled by, missing him by inches. His friend Salvatore rushed over.

3   "Hey, that was close," Salvatore said, offering him a grimy hand to help him up. "Come on, we need a break."

4   Jedrek looked around. "But the foreman . . ." he began.

5   "He won't notice us," Salvatore replied. "Come on."

Children working in a textile factory

                    © *Shell Education*

Bread and Roses *(cont.)*

6   The small boy threw his weight against a heavy wooden door. Jedrek followed him, and they slipped through the opening. It was slightly quieter in the storeroom, so they didn't have to shout over the roaring looms in the factory. Salvatore sat down on a bale of cloth.

7   Although Jedrek was 11, a year older than Salvatore, he looked up to the younger boy. Salvatore had been working at the textile mill longer, ever since he'd entered the United States.

8   "I bet you wish you was back in school," Salvatore said.

9   "I sure do, but my folks need the money I earn," Jedrek said with a shrug. "What about you? Did you go to school back in Italy?"

10 "Of course I went to school," Salvatore replied. "Then we came here because my pa thought we were going to be rich in America. Instead we all have to work just to make ends meet. At least I'm learning to read English."

11 "Yeah?"

12 "Yeah, take a look."

13 Salvatore reached into his trousers pocket and pulled out a crumpled piece of paper. Jedrek held it up to the dim light from the grime-smeared window and saw that it had writing in six different languages. The part in English read, "We demand bread and roses!"

14 "I read the Italian part, then the English part," Salvatore stated. "I'm not sure what 'bread and roses' means. Do you know?"

15 "It means textile workers need more than better pay," Jedrek explained. "It means we want a decent life. We want to work in safer conditions."

16 Salvatore stood up, took the paper from Jedrek, and folded it carefully. "Sounds good to me. Well, maybe someday, but now we'd better get back to work, before the foreman notices we're missing."

17 They pushed open the door and returned to the roaring machines.

Name: _____ Date: _____

Bread and Roses (cont.)

Directions: Fill in the bubble of each correct answer choice.

1. Which answer choice best explains the slogan "bread and roses"?

   Ⓐ eating sandwiches and planting flowers

   Ⓑ providing safer work conditions and earning more money

   Ⓒ working with friends and being with family

   Ⓓ buying expensive houses and taking long vacations

2. Read this sentence from the story: ". . . so they didn't have to shout over the roaring looms in the factory." What is the meaning of *looms* as it is used in the story?

   Ⓐ doors

   Ⓑ buildings

   Ⓒ factories

   Ⓓ machines

3. What can the reader conclude about looms based on the sentence in number 2?

   Ⓔ They are small.

   Ⓕ They are very noisy.

   Ⓖ They are old.

   Ⓗ They are inexpensive.

Bread and Roses (cont.)

Directions: Fill in the bubble of each correct answer choice.

4. Which feature in the photograph helps to explain the workers' demand for bread and roses?

   Ⓐ wood floors

   Ⓑ barefoot workers

   Ⓒ spools of thread

   Ⓓ large machines

5. Which sentence shows how Salvatore's life in America differs from what his father had pictured?

   Ⓐ "At least I'm learning to read English."

   Ⓑ "I bet you wish you was back in school."

   Ⓒ "Instead we all have to work just to make ends meet."

   Ⓓ "It means textile workers need more than better pay."

6. What can the reader conclude about Salvatore?

   Ⓐ He does not attend school in America.

   Ⓑ He is jealous and dislikes Jedrek.

   Ⓒ He is working to save money for himself.

   Ⓓ He has known Jedrek his whole life.

Name: _____ Date: _____

Bread and Roses *(cont.)*

Directions: Answer the questions.

7. Complete the Venn diagram with information about Salvatore and Jedrek.

Salvatore   **Jedrek**

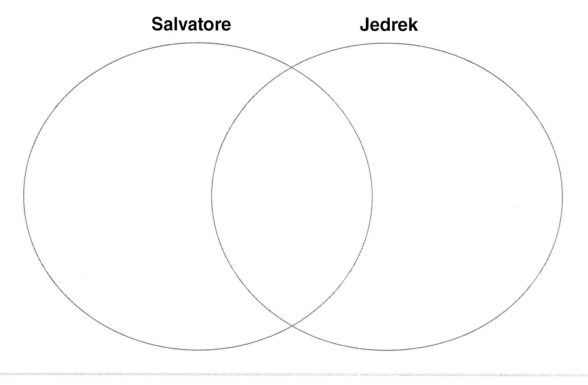

8. Summarize the information from the Venn diagram above into one paragraph to describe the similarities and differences between Jedrek and Salvatore.

_____

_____

_____

_____

_____

Name: _____   Date: _____

The Cause of the Mutiny

from *Tarzan of the Apes* by Edgar Rice Burroughs

Directions: Read this story and respond to the questions on pages 59–61.

1   Two sailors were washing the decks of the *Fuwalda*. The first mate was on duty. The captain had stopped to speak with two passengers, Lord John and Lady Alice Greystoke. They were facing away from the sailors. The men were working backwards toward the little group. Closer and closer the workers came until one of them was right behind the captain. In another moment he would have passed by, and then this strange tale would not have been written. But just then, the captain turned to leave Lord John and Lady Alice. As he did so, he tripped against the sailor. The captain sprawled face first upon the deck. He overturned the water pail, too, and was drenched in its dirty contents.

2   The captain's face darkened with the scarlet of rage. The captain got to his feet. With a terrific blow, he knocked the sailor to the deck. The man was small and rather old, which made the brutality of the act even more shocking. The other sailor was neither old nor small. He was a huge bear of a man. He had a fierce black mustache and a great bull neck set between massive shoulders. As he saw his mate go down, he crouched. With a snarl, he sprang upon the captain and crushed him to his knees with one mighty blow.

These ships are like the Fuwalda.

The Cause of the Mutiny (cont.)

3   The captain's face changed from scarlet to white. This was mutiny! This captain had met and stopped mutiny before in his career. Without rising, he whipped a gun from his pocket. He fired point blank at the great mountain of muscle towering before him. But, quick as he was, John was almost as quick. The bullet meant for the sailor's heart lodged in his leg instead. Lord Greystoke had struck down the captain's arm when he saw the gun flash in the sun.

4   Angry words passed between John and the captain. John made it plain that he was disgusted with the brutality displayed toward the crew. He would not tolerate anything further of the kind while he and Lady Greystoke were passengers. The captain was on the point of making an angry reply. Thinking better of it, he turned on his heel. Scowling, he strode away. He did not dare to anger an English official. The queen's mighty arm wielded an instrument, which he feared—England's navy.

5   The two sailors picked themselves up. The older man assisted his wounded mate to rise. The big fellow tried his leg gingerly. Finding that it bore his weight, he turned to John with a gruff word of thanks. Though the fellow's tone was surly, his words were clearly well meant.

Life at sea was very difficult.

The Cause of the Mutiny *(cont.)*

Directions: Fill in the bubble of each correct answer choice.

1. What sentence from the story best completes this diagram?

Cause		Effect
		He tripped and fell face first on the deck.

Ⓐ "With a snarl, he sprang upon the captain and crushed him to his knees with one mighty blow."

Ⓑ "But just then, the captain turned to leave Lord John and Lady Alice."

Ⓒ "Lord Greystoke had struck down the captain's arm when he saw the gun flash in the sun."

Ⓓ "The men were working backwards toward the little group."

2. Read this sentence from paragraph 2: "The captain's face darkened with the scarlet of rage." Why does the author include this sentence?

Ⓐ to show how bruised and swollen the captain is

Ⓑ to show how displeased the captain is with the first mate's work

Ⓒ to describe the captain's reaction to being embarrassed

Ⓓ to give details about what the weather is like

3. What two details from the story help support the answer to number 2?

Ⓔ "He overturned the water pail, too, and was drenched in its dirty contents."

Ⓕ "John made it plain that he was disgusted with the brutality displayed toward the crew."

Ⓖ "The captain sprawled face first upon the deck."

Ⓗ "He fired point blank at the great mountain of muscle towering before him."

Name: _____ Date: _____

The Cause of the Mutiny (cont.)

Directions: Fill in the bubble of each correct answer choice.

Read this dictionary entry for *mutiny*.

mutiny \'myü-tə-nē\; noun

1. a situation in which a group of sailors refuse to obey orders and try to take control away from the one who commands them

4. What sentence from the story convinces the captain that *mutiny* has occurred?

   Ⓐ "As he saw his mate go down, he crouched"

   Ⓑ "Scowling, he strode away."

   Ⓒ "The older man assisted his wounded mate to rise."

   Ⓓ "With a snarl, he sprang upon the captain and crushed him to his knees with one mighty blow."

5. Reread paragraph 4. What two details from the story indicate the captain's reason for avoiding any conflict with John?

   Ⓐ "Angry words passed between John and the captain."

   Ⓑ "He did not dare to anger an English official."

   Ⓒ "Scowling, he strode away."

   Ⓓ "The queen's mighty arm wielded an instrument, which he feared— England's navy."

6. Which event from the story is based solely on the captain's opinion?

   Ⓐ the captain's response to the sailors' behavior

   Ⓑ the captain's collision with the small, old sailor

   Ⓒ the argument between the captain and Lord Greystroke

   Ⓓ the captain's fear of angering Lord Greystroke

Name: _____ Date: _____

The Cause of the Mutiny *(cont.)*

Directions: Answer the questions.

7. What kind of a person is the captain? Support your answer with at least two details from the story.

    _____

    _____

    _____

    _____

    _____

8. What does the reader learn about Lord John Greystroke in this story? Write a personality trait in each of the boxes below. Then, write evidence from the text to explain each trait.

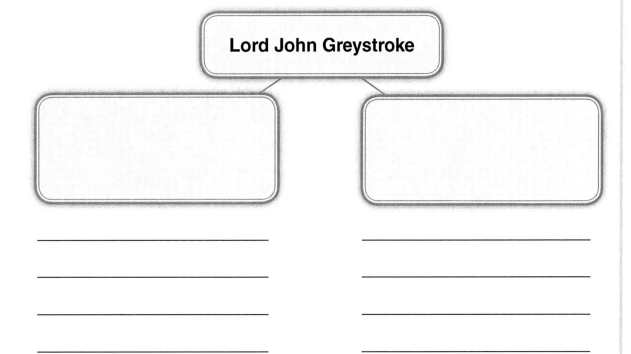

Name: _____ Date: _____

Mr. Nobody
by Anonymous

Directions: Read this poem and respond to the questions on pages 63–65.

1   I know a funny little man who's as quiet as a mouse,
Who does the mischief that is done in everybody's house!
There's no one ever sees his face, and yet we all agree
That every plate we break was cracked by Mr. Nobody.

5   'Tis he who always tears our books, who leaves the door ajar,
He pulls the buttons from our shirts and scatters pins afar.
That squeaking door will always squeak—forever! 'Cause you see
We leave its oiling to be done by Mr. Nobody.

9   The fingerprints upon the door by none of us are made.
We never leave the blinds unclosed to let the curtains fade.
The milk we never spill; the boots that lying 'round you see
Are not our boots! They all belong to Mr. Nobody.

Name: _____   Date: _____

Mr. Nobody *(cont.)*

Directions: Fill in the bubble of each correct answer choice.

1. Which line from the poem explains the purpose of Mr. Nobody?

    Ⓐ "Are not our boots! They all belong to Mr. Nobody."

    Ⓑ "I know a funny little man who's as quiet as a mouse"

    Ⓒ "There's no one ever sees his face, and yet we all agree"

    Ⓓ "Who does the mischief that is done in everybody's house!"

2. In which line does the author refuse to accept responsibility?

    Ⓐ "I know a funny little man who's as quiet as a mouse."

    Ⓑ "The fingerprints upon the door by none of us are made."

    Ⓒ "That squeaking door will always squeak—forever! 'Cause you see"

    Ⓓ "Who does the mischief that is done in everybody's house!"

3. Which line from the poem best supports the idea that Mr. Nobody is imaginary?

    Ⓐ line 1

    Ⓑ line 3

    Ⓒ line 8

    Ⓓ line 12

Name: _____ Date: _____

Mr. Nobody (cont.)

Directions: Fill in the bubble of each correct answer choice.

4. Which of the five senses allows the reader to best imagine what occurs in line 7?

   Ⓐ seeing

   Ⓑ smelling

   Ⓒ tasting

   Ⓓ hearing

5. Which other detail from the poem serves a similar purpose?

   Ⓔ "We never leave the blinds unclosed to let the curtains fade."

   Ⓕ "The milk we never spill; the boots that lying 'round you see"

   Ⓖ "I know a funny little man who's as quiet as a mouse"

   Ⓗ "He pulls the buttons from our shirts and scatters pins afar."

6. Which statements are facts about the poem, "Mr. Nobody"? There is more than one correct response.

   Ⓐ There is a rhyming pattern in the poem.

   Ⓑ There are 12 stanzas in the poem.

   Ⓒ Each line ends with punctuation.

   Ⓓ Each stanza consists of four lines.

Name: _____ Date: _____

Mr. Nobody (cont.)

Directions: Answer the questions.

7. How is Mr. Nobody similar to a young child? Use at least three examples from the poem to support your answer.

_____

_____

_____

_____

8. Complete the graphic organizer with details from the poem that tell about the mischief caused by Mr. Nobody.

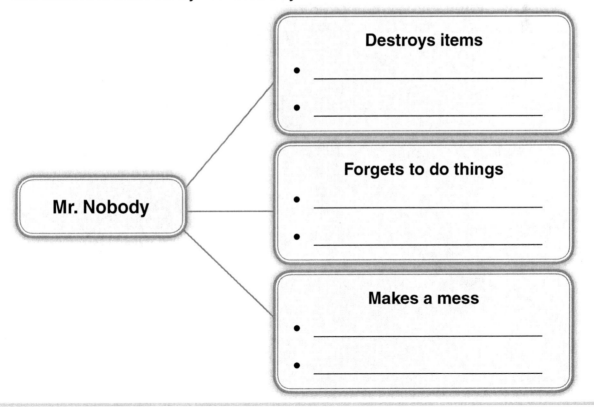

Destroys items
- _____
- _____

Forgets to do things
- _____
- _____

Makes a mess
- _____
- _____

Mr. Nobody

Poetry Practice Exercise

The Sun's Travels
by Robert Louis Stevenson

Directions: Read this poem and respond to the questions on pages 67–69.

1   The sun is not in bed when I
At night upon my pillow lie.
Still 'round the earth his way he takes,
And morning after morning makes.

5   While here at home, in shining day,
We 'round the sunny garden play,
Each little Indian sleepyhead
Is being kissed and put in bed.

9   And when at eve I rise from tea,
Day dawns beyond the Atlantic Sea.
And all the children in the West
Are getting up and being dressed.

Name: _____ Date: _____

The Sun's Travels (cont.)

Directions: Fill in the bubble of each correct answer choice.

1. Which line from the poem lets the reader know it is nighttime for the author?

   Ⓐ "Each little Indian sleepyhead"

   Ⓑ "Day dawns beyond the Atlantic Sea."

   Ⓒ "At night upon my pillow lie."

   Ⓓ "We 'round the sunny garden play"

2. What idea is the author expressing in the poem?

   Ⓐ The author is always traveling to be in daylight.

   Ⓑ Somewhere it is always the opposite time of day from where the author is.

   Ⓒ The sun appears at the same time of day for everyone around the world.

   Ⓓ Nighttime is the best part of the author's day.

3. Which lines from the poem best support the answer to number 2?

   Ⓔ lines 1 and 2

   Ⓕ lines 3 and 4

   Ⓖ lines 5 and 6

   Ⓗ lines 7 and 8

Name: _____   Date: _____

The Sun's Travels (cont.)

Directions: Fill in the bubble of each correct answer choice.

4. In which line does the author personify the sun?

ⓐ line 3

ⓑ line 6

ⓒ line 10

ⓓ line 12

5. Which line helps the reader to infer where the author lives?

ⓐ "Are getting up and being dressed."

ⓑ "The sun is not in bed when I"

ⓒ "Is being kissed and put in bed."

ⓓ "And all the children in the West"

6. Which is true about the poem?

ⓐ There is no punctuation used in the poem.

ⓑ All of the lines rhyme with each other.

ⓒ Some of the lines are incomplete sentences.

ⓓ Only a few lines start with a capital letter.

Name: _____   Date: _____

The Sun's Travels (cont.)

Directions: Answer the questions.

7. Below is a parallel poem to "The Sun's Travels." This parallel poem is based on the format and topic of Stevenson's poem. Compare the poems.

> **The Moon's Travels**
> By fourth grader Kiley Smith
>
> 1 The moon is not asleep when I
> Open up my sleepy eyes.
> He travels Earth 'round and again
> And night after night I see my friend.
>
> 5 While here at home, in mystical night,
> We're snuggled up with eyes closed tight.
> Each little German wakes as one
> And looks forward to a day of fun
>
> 9 And when I get up out of bed
> Somewhere in the back of my head
> I know the children in the East
> Are finishing their evening feasts

Name a similarity:	Name a similarity:	Name a difference:

Drama Practice Exercise

Two Flat Friends Travel the World
by Wendy Conklin

Directions: Read this script and respond to the questions on pages 73–75.

Willie and Fred have a school assignment to learn about different countries. After reading the book Flat Stanley, *they decide to flatten themselves and travel the world through the mail. They meet a girl named Eman in Egypt.*

1   **Eman**: It's not often that I get anything in the mail. I opened the envelope and reached inside.

Willie: Somebody had hold of my ten flat toes!

Fred: She pulled us out and introduced herself.

Eman: Never had I seen a sight like the one I saw that day! Their bodies were so flat that I knew they had to be hungry. I gave them thick hummus dip and pita bread. Then we took a bus to see Egypt's amazing sites. The pyramids were first!

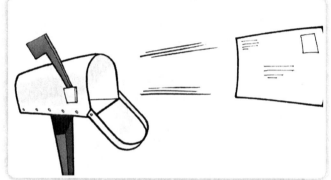

5   **Willie**: We could see the massive structures from far away.

Eman: One of the pyramids took 23 years to build!

Fred: Great kings called pharaohs are buried there. Each pharaoh was made into a mummy, wrapped in cloth, and placed inside a sarcophagus.

Willie: The pharaohs buried their gold with them, too.

Eman: They believed the gold and treasures would be needed during the afterlife.

10   **Willie**: It's no wonder there were people who broke into the pyramids to rob the tombs.

Eman: A massive stone sphinx sits nearby, too. A sphinx is an imaginary creature that is half lion and half man.

Fred: He looks like he is guarding the pyramids.

Eman: We saw how the ancient Egyptians wrote, too.

Two Flat Friends Travel the World (cont.)

Willie: But this didn't look like our writing.

15 **Fred**: Instead of using words, they used pictures called hieroglyphics.

Eman: The walls of the pyramids are covered with this picture writing. Years ago, someone discovered how to read hieroglyphics.

Fred: That helped people learn what life was like in ancient Egypt.

Eman: I also took them to see the Nile, the longest river in the world.

Willie: I couldn't believe it stretches for 1,450 kilometers. That's 900 miles!

20 **Fred**: Willie and I had a super time with Eman as our guide.

Eman: Then it was time for them to visit other lands.

Willie: We squeezed in a hug as she slid us into our envelope.

Fred: She had to be careful not to wrinkle my legs.

Eman: I was sad to see them leave, but I knew they had more research to do. I mailed them to China.

25 **Mazu**: I found an envelope in my mailbox. Guess what I heard? Talking!

Fred: Imagine how he felt when he slid us out and saw that we were two kids! We told him that we were on a quest to see the amazing sites of China.

Mazu: In that case, allow me to be your guide!

Willie: What are some interesting sites to see here?

Mazu: You may have heard about our amazing long wall? Everyone calls it the Great Wall of China.

30 **Fred and Willie**: The Great Wall of China is a fantastic place to start!

Two Flat Friends Travel the World (cont.)

Willie: The Great Wall is more than 1,600 kilometers long. That's over 1,000 miles.

Mazu: It has a wide path on top. In some places, the path is wide enough for five horses to ride side by side!

Fred: Legends say that it took 10 years to build.

Mazu: I also took them to see a clay army made for a powerful ruler. The army is called the Terra-cotta Warriors.

35 **Willie**: The ruler thought his army would protect him after he died.

Fred: The clay men in this army are life-size.

Mazu: Each soldier is unique, and every face is different.

Willie: There are even clay horses in the army.

Fred: And don't forget the chariots! There are 7,500 clay men, horses, and chariots in all.

40 **Mazu**: That may sound like a lot, but this ruler's real army was much bigger.

Fred: Hundreds of years ago, a palace was built.

Mazu: People could only go there if the emperor invited them. The palace was called the Forbidden City.

Willie: We had Mazu take pictures of us in front of the palace.

Mazu: Did you know that the ancient Chinese carried their emperors on litters?

45 **Fred**: What's a litter?

Mazu: A litter is a chair that could be carried around.

Fred: The time had come for Willie and me to go home.

Willie: We couldn't have asked for a better guide in China than Mazu!

Name: _____   Date: _____

Two Flat Friends Travel the World (cont.)

Directions: Fill in the bubble of each correct answer choice.

1. The author most likely wrote this script to . . .
   Ⓐ give the reader a summary of the book *Flat Stanley*.
   Ⓑ present historical facts in an entertaining way.
   Ⓒ give the reader as much information about China as possible.
   Ⓓ show interactions between characters with meaningful dialogue.

2. Which two sentences from the script are facts about Egypt?
   Ⓐ "In some places, the path is wide enough for five horses to ride side by side!"
   Ⓑ "The army is called the Terra-cotta Warriors."
   Ⓒ "They believed the gold and treasures would be needed during the afterlife."
   Ⓓ "I also took them to see the Nile, the longest river in the world."

3. How might this script be similar to a nonfiction article about Egypt and China?
   Ⓐ They both present facts.
   Ⓑ They both have lively characters.
   Ⓒ They both have narrators.
   Ⓓ The dialogue entertains the reader.

Name: _____ Date: _____

Two Flat Friends Travel the World (cont.)

Directions: Fill in the bubble of each correct answer choice.

4. What purpose does the character Mazu serve in this script?

   Ⓐ Mazu provides comic relief for the reader.

   Ⓑ Mazu's personality is comforting to the reader.

   Ⓒ Mazu presents historical facts to the reader.

   Ⓓ Mazu allows the reader to predict what will happen next.

5. What statement supports the answer to number 4?

   Ⓔ "I found an envelope in my mailbox. Guess what I heard? Talking!"

   Ⓕ "Did you know that the ancient Chinese carried their emperors on litters?"

   Ⓖ "In that case, allow me to be your guide!"

   Ⓗ "We couldn't have asked for a better guide in China than Mazu!"

6. What fact about China is supported by the script?

   Ⓐ The Great Wall of China took over 100 years to construct.

   Ⓑ The Forbidden City was always a place anyone could visit.

   Ⓒ A ruler used life-size clay soldiers to protect him after death.

   Ⓓ The Great Wall of China is wide enough for 1,600 people to walk side-by-side.

Name: _____   Date: _____

Two Flat Friends Travel the World (cont.)

Directions: Answer the questions.

7. Use the text to complete the chart. Mark the correct country for each item.

Item	Egypt	China
pharaohs		
Terra-cotta Warriors		
pyramids		
emperors		
sphinx		
Nile		
Great Wall		
hieroglyphics		
mummies		
Forbidden City		

8. Choose either Egypt or China and explain the aspects of life in that country that are described in the text. Use the text for specific examples.

_____

_____

_____

_____

_____

Name: _____ Date: _____

Life in a Continental Camp
by Kathleen E. Bradley

Directions: Read this script and respond to the questions on pages 79–81.

The script takes place during the Revolutionary War. The action peaks at the battle of Monmouth in New Jersey in June 1778.

1 **Private**: General Washington, the redcoats are marching to New York!

Washington: We must stop them! Private, gather my generals.

Private: Yes, sir!

Narrator: A meeting is held at Valley Forge to discuss battle plans. Major General Charles Lee, Washington's senior officer, is quick to voice his doubts about a full attack.

5 **Lee**: General Washington, our troops lack the skills to fight the world's finest army.

Washington: Our army has received special training.

Lee: The British have more troops. They were well cared for this past winter. Our troops barely survived the cold, hunger, and disease that were here.

Washington: You don't know my soldiers' hardships!

Lee: I know that a full attack is unwise at this point. We should send small parties to sabotage the British.

Washington: I disagree. We will pursue the army and engage them in a full attack. Gather your men and prepare to depart!

10 **Lee**: Yes, sir.

Life in a Continental Camp *(cont.)*

	Narrator:	Across the field, Molly "Pitcher" Hays sits under a tree. Her white ruffled cap is pushed back on her head. She sews a soldier's shirt. Her husband, William, sits nearby.
	William:	Molly, we have received orders to move out of Valley Forge today.
	Narrator:	Molly looks up. She spits the needle that is in her mouth squarely into her pincushion. Then she thrusts the cushion into her pocket like a soldier returning his sword to its case.
	Molly:	Leaving? When I still have a hundred uniforms to sew?
15	**William**:	Those are the orders. No use complaining, soldier.
	Molly:	All right then, let me feed your empty stomachs. Listen for the bell.
	Narrator:	Molly travels with the army. She sews and cooks for the soldiers. She prepares breakfast and rings the bell.
	Private:	Last one in line goes without breakfast!
	Molly:	Okay, boys, line up. Shoulders back. Dishes face up!
20	**William**:	Yes, ma'am!
	Molly:	I will not have my firecakes and eggs dropped on this muddy field.
	William:	Yes, but . . . firecakes? Molly, why did you go and bake those? Once Congress sent us food, I thought we'd never be forced to eat them again!
	Private:	I agree! They're awful.
	Narrator:	Molly has a glint in her eye as she wipes her arm across her forehead.
25	**Molly**:	Awful, eh? Do my ears deceive me?
	Private:	Pardon me, ma'am, but all the firecakes that I have eaten were as hard as musket balls and . . .
	William:	Watch your step, son, and tread lightly.

Life in a Continental Camp (cont.)

	Narrator:	Molly grabs one of her firecake biscuits. She pretends to wind up for a fierce pitch at the young private.
	William:	Molly! The young man was just stating his opinion. Isn't that one of the reasons we're fighting this war?
30	**Molly:**	Yes, William. Thankfully, I am feeling patriotic this morning, so I will spare the boy. All right then, who's hungry?
	William:	We all are!
	Molly:	Very well. Man your plates!
	Narrator:	Then, with the agility of a circus performer, Molly grabs dozens of eggs from the basket beside her. With her left hand, she tosses them into the air, one by one, juggling them in a circle above her head. As each egg falls into her right hand, she cracks it before it lands perfectly in the hot frying pan.
	Private:	Molly, these are the finest scrambled eggs ever.
35	**Molly:**	Of course! My juggling scrambles them before the yolks hit the pan!
	Narrator:	Soon after, the Continental Army packs up and moves out. General Washington meets with his officers.
	Washington:	Gentlemen, General Lee will attack the rear flank of the British army. An equal army will circle around and attack the front.
	Lee:	The British have more troops! I warn you, this strategy is sure to fail.
	Washington:	The spirit of this army cannot fail.
40	**Lee:**	But, sir, no amount of spirit will make up for the lack of soldiers!
	Washington:	There is nothing worse than a commander unsure about his troops. General Lafayette, will you lead the attack?
	Lee:	Step back, Lafayette. You're nothing but a boy. I won't give up this mission to a lesser man.
	Washington:	Very well, General Lee. Plan your attack.

#51437—TIME For Kids: Practicing for Today's Tests

© Shell Education

Name: _____   Date: _____

Life in a Continental Camp *(cont.)*

Directions: Fill in the bubble of each correct answer choice.

1. What does General Washington say that shows he is unsure of General Lee's ability to take command?

    Ⓐ "General Lafayette, will you lead the attack?"

    Ⓑ "The spirit of this army cannot fail."

    Ⓒ "We must stop them! Private, gather my generals."

    Ⓓ "Very well, General Lee. Plan your attack!"

2. What did General Lee say to make Washington uncertain regarding Lee's commitment?

    Ⓔ "General Washington, our troops lack the skills to fight the world's finest army."

    Ⓕ "We should send small parties to sabotage the British."

    Ⓖ "But, sir, no amount of spirit will make up for the lack of soldiers!"

    Ⓗ "I know that a full attack is unwise at this point."

3. Which detail from the script lets the reader conclude that Molly has a temper?

    Ⓐ "Those are the orders. No use complaining, soldier."

    Ⓑ "Okay, boys, line up. Shoulders back. Dishes face up!"

    Ⓒ "Last one in line goes without breakfast!"

    Ⓓ "Molly! The young man was just stating his opinion."

Name: _____   Date: _____

Life in a Continental Camp (cont.)

Directions: Fill in the bubble of each correct answer choice.

4. Why does the author include a narrator in this script?

   Ⓐ There are not enough characters.

   Ⓑ The narrator was there during the actual event.

   Ⓒ Every script includes a narrator.

   Ⓓ The narrator explains things that would be hard to include as conversation.

5. Which phrase supports the author's idea that Molly is as agile as a circus performer?

   Ⓐ "She spits the needle that is in her mouth squarely into her pincushion."

   Ⓑ "She pretends to wind up for a fierce pitch at the young private."

   Ⓒ "As each egg falls into her right hand, she cracks it before it lands perfectly in the hot frying pan."

   Ⓓ "Then she thrusts the cushion into her pocket like a soldier returning his sword to its case."

6. Read this sentence from line 37: "Gentlemen, General Lee will attack the rear flank of the British army." What is the meaning of *flank* as used in this statement?

   Ⓐ the side of an animal between the ribs and hips

   Ⓑ a side of a military formation

   Ⓒ the side of a mountain

   Ⓓ a side of beef

Name: _____ Date: _____

Life in a Continental Camp *(cont.)*

Directions: Answer the questions.

7. Use the text to complete this Venn diagram comparing and contrasting Molly "Pitcher" Hays and George Washington. Put two details in each section.

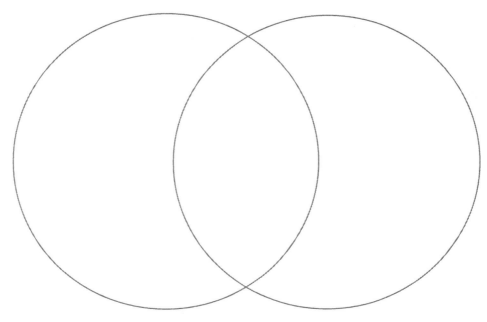

Molly "Pitcher" Hays   **George Washington**

8. Choose either Molly "Pitcher" Hays or George Washington. Using details from the text, describe how he or she plays an important role in life at the Continental Army camp.

_____

_____

_____

_____

_____

Name: _____   Date: _____

John Henry
by Dona Herweck Rice

Directions: Read this script and respond to the questions on pages 85–87.

During the late 1800s, John Henry, a former slave, gets a job hammering stakes to lay railroad tracks. His strength and determination make him an unstoppable worker for the Chesapeake and Ohio railroad company.

1 **Worker 1**: John Henry was a mighty, steel-driving man. He drove steel across this great country for the Chesapeake and Ohio Railroad—otherwise known as the C&O. Miles of track were laid so that trains called iron horses could ride them across the land. I worked on those rails, and I saw firsthand the work that John could do.

Worker 2: I worked those lines as well. It took incredible strength and endurance to stand in all kinds of weather hammering the huge iron stakes that hold the rails in place. But wait a minute—the C&O is not where John's story starts!

Polly Ann: Oh, no. This story begins on the day of jubilation—the day when John, his ma, and I were set free.

Worker 1: You see, John's mother was born into slavery.

5 **Worker 2**: And so were John and Polly Ann.

Ma: The slave master forced John to work so hard!

Polly Ann: Oh, my, how they worked him! He was tall and broad shouldered—an awesome powerhouse of a man!

Ma: They worked him hard—yes, they did. But they chained him, too, because he was so strong that the slave master feared him.

Polly Ann: They chained him just like you would a ferocious animal!

10 **Worker 1**: But the day of emancipation came at last . . .

Ma: And we were all freed! We could hardly believe it was true and that now we could make our own way.

Polly Ann: John swore he would never wear chains again.

Ma: And so we melted down his chains and forged them into a huge hammer.

    © Shell Education

John Henry *(cont.)*

Polly Ann: It was a hammer as mighty as John.

15 **Worker 2:** And John said . . .

John Henry: This hammer feels just right in my hand. But, Polly Ann, I think it may be the death of me one day. One day I'll die with this hammer in my hand.

Polly Ann: Don't you say that, John. Truth is, we're going to live by that hammer. We'll be together, John, and that hammer will make us a new life.

Worker 1: John embraced Polly Ann then and there, and the two of them were married just days later. John found a way to use that hammer to make a new life for himself and his wife.

John Henry: Polly Ann, I'm going to work for the railroad! With this hammer, I can drive steel as well as any man. What do you say?

20 **Polly Ann:** I say yes, John, I'm with you, and I know you'll drive steel better than any other man.

John Henry: Ma, you'll have a home with us, too. Will you come?

Ma: I'd be mighty glad to, John.

Worker 2: And so the trio headed to West Virginia where John took a job with the C&O and became a steel-driving man.

Worker 1: When I first saw John, I couldn't help but stare, for he was something to behold!

25 **Worker 2:** Now, you've heard that John was a strong, mighty man, but the truth is, he was a mountain of a man! When he first walked into our railroad work camp, that mountain blocked the sun!

Worker 1: That's the truth. I looked up from my work and just saw muscles silhouetted against the shimmering sun.

Worker 2: Then the boss called out . . .

Boss: Hey there, mister, are you looking for work?

John Henry: Yes, that's right. I'm looking to build railroads.

John Henry *(cont.)*

30 **Boss**: Well, you've come to the right place. What's your experience?

John Henry: None but a lifetime of hard work, and I can wield this hammer as well as any man can.

Boss: We'll see about that. I take only the best on my railroad, so let's see what you can do. You workers there, take this fellow to the end of the line and show him what to do. I'll be watching.

Worker 1: Yes, Boss, we'll show him the ropes.

Worker 2: You sure do have the brawn, but can you wield that hammer with a steady blow?

35 **John Henry**: Just you watch—stand back!

Ma: John lifted his hammer high above his head.

Polly Ann: Down he swung with one mighty blow! That's all it took him to drive a steel spike through the rail to fasten it in place. No iron horse, no matter how fast or heavy, could rip that steel spike loose. None of the other workers were capable of such a feat; it took them many hammer blows to secure each spike.

Worker 1: Did you see that? Just one blow!

Worker 2: And you've never done this work before? That's unbelievable!

40 **John Henry**: It's a fact, but my ma says that I was born with a hammer in my hand.

Boss: Henry, you've got the job. Now let's get this railroad built—everyone back to work!

John Henry *(cont.)*

Directions: Fill in the bubble of the correct answer choice.

1. Which phrase from the text helps explain why John was put in chains?

    Ⓐ "were set free"

    Ⓑ "a hammer as mighty as John"

    Ⓒ "he was so strong"

    Ⓓ "forced John to work"

2. Which character's speech helps the reader understand what the word *emancipation* means?

    Ⓐ Ma

    Ⓑ Polly Ann

    Ⓒ John Henry

    Ⓓ Worker 2

3. Which element of a play is present in this script?

    Ⓐ a narrator

    Ⓑ a list of props

    Ⓒ stage directions

    Ⓓ dialogue

Name: _____   Date: _____

John Henry *(cont.)*

Directions: Fill in the bubble of each correct answer choice.

4. Read this sentence from line 26: "I looked up from my work and just saw muscles silhouetted against the shimmering sun." What does this tell us about John Henry?

   Ⓐ He dreams that he will be struck with a hammer and die.

   Ⓑ He is larger and stronger than most men.

   Ⓒ His muscles were round like the sun.

   Ⓓ His shadow is hard to make out.

5. What other detail from the text helps support the answer to number 4?

   Ⓔ ". . . that mountain blocked the sun!"

   Ⓕ "I can wield this hammer as well as any man can."

   Ⓖ "Henry, you've got the job."

   Ⓗ "John took a job with the C&O and became a steel-driving man."

6. As spoken by Polly Ann at the end of the script, what does the word *blow* mean?

   Ⓐ a violent windstorm

   Ⓑ to move air

   Ⓒ a sudden, hard strike

   Ⓓ to give out sound

John Henry *(cont.)*

Directions: Answer the questions.

7. Draw a line to match each character to something he or she says in the script.

Characters

Polly Ann

Boss

Worker 2

John Henry

Worker 1

Ma

Quotation

"Well, you've come to the right place."

"They worked him hard—yes, they did."

"I couldn't help but stare, for he was something to behold!"

"This story begins on the day of jubilation . . . ."

"That's unbelievable!"

"This hammer feels just right in my hand."

8. Why is John Henry successful as a C&O railroad worker? Use at least two details from the text to support your response.

_____

_____

_____

_____

Name: _____   Date: _____

The Lion
by Mary Howitt

Directions: Read this poem and respond to the questions on page 89.

1   When Lion sends his roaring forth,
    Silence falls upon the earth.
    For all creatures, great and small
    Know his terror-breathing call.

5   And, as if by death pursued,
    Leave him to his solitude.
    Lion, you are made to dwell
    In hot lands, intractable.
    And yourself, the sun, the sand

10 Are a tyrannous triple band.
    Lion-king and desert throne,
    All the region is your own!

The Lion *(cont.)*

Directions: Fill in the bubble of each correct answer choice.

1. What is the first stanza mainly about?

   Ⓐ what a lion looks like

   Ⓑ the sound a lion makes

   Ⓒ where a lion lives

   Ⓓ what a lion eats

2. What detail from the poem provides evidence to support the answer to number 1?

   Ⓔ "In hot lands, intractable."

   Ⓕ "Leave him to his solitude."

   Ⓖ "Know his terror-breathing call."

   Ⓗ "Are a tyrannous triple band."

3. Which line in the poem supports the idea that a lion is like royalty?

   Ⓐ line 3

   Ⓑ line 4

   Ⓒ line 9

   Ⓓ line 11

Name: _____ Date: _____

A Big Home for Big Cats

Directions: Read this text and respond to the questions on page 91.

1   What would the world be like if there were no more wild tigers? Sadly, that day may soon be here. The number of wild tigers is dropping. One hundred years ago, about 100,000 tigers roamed Asia. Now there are less than 3,000.

2   What is killing the tigers? People. It's against the law to hunt them. Yet humans still do so. Plus, people ruin tigers' habitats. The forests, jungles, and swamps where tigers live are being cut down. People are building roads, farms, and towns.

Big Cats in Trouble

3   Tigers aren't the only wild cats in trouble. Most of the world's big cats face threats. This includes lions, jaguars, cheetahs, and snow leopards. All big cats need lots of space to roam. This brings them into conflict with the ever-growing human population.

4   Even inside a wildlife park, big cats aren't always safe. Illegal hunters sneak inside. And cats in parks are sometimes hit by disease. In 1994, one-third of all the lions in a park in Tanzania died from a virus. Even more lions died in another game park in 2001. This time the deaths were due to a tick-borne parasite. And if a big cat gets canine distemper, it is a death sentence. Distemper is a sickness that kills dogs. Pets get shots to protect them from it.

The World's Biggest Reserve

5   Animal lovers around the world want to save big cats. One solution is to set aside more land for them. Myanmar is a country in Asia. It started the world's largest tiger reserve. It is the size of the state of Vermont. Today about 150 tigers live there. Wildlife workers hope that number will grow to 1,000.

6   Alan Rabinowitz works for the World Conservation Society. He says that tigers born in the park can be brought to other areas where tigers have died out. This way the tiger population will spread out.

7   Thanks to reserves like this one, we can hope there will always be tigers running free.

A Big Home for Big Cats (cont.)

Directions: Fill in the bubble of each correct answer choice.

4. What country borders the Hukawng Valley Tiger Reserve?

- Ⓐ China
- Ⓑ Thailand
- Ⓒ Laos
- Ⓓ India

5. What sentence from the article supports the author's argument that wildlife parks aren't always safe for big cats?

- Ⓐ "And if a big cat gets canine distemper, it is a death sentence."
- Ⓑ "The forests, jungles, and swamps where tigers live are being cut down."
- Ⓒ "People are building roads, farms, and towns."
- Ⓓ "The number of wild tigers is dropping."

Read this dictionary entry for the word *reserve*.

reserve \ri-ˈzərv\

verb
1. to keep back or save for future use

noun
2. area of land set apart for a special purpose
3. a member of a team who plays if another player drops out
4. cash held aside by a company to meet demands

6. Which meaning of *reserve* is used in paragraph 5?

- Ⓐ meaning 1
- Ⓑ meaning 2
- Ⓒ meaning 3
- Ⓓ meaning 4

Name: _____   Date: _____

The Lion and A Big Home for Big Cats

Directions: Reread the texts on pages 88 and 90, and fill in the bubble of each correct answer choice.

7. What is one difference between the article and the poem?

    Ⓐ The article tells the reader that big cats are safe, while the poem says they are dangerous.

    Ⓑ In the article, lions aren't mentioned. In the poem they are.

    Ⓒ The article mentions different big cats, while the poem focuses on one.

    Ⓓ In the article, protecting the animals is important. In the poem, capturing them is important.

8. What can the reader infer from both the poem and the article?

    Ⓐ Large cats are nearly extinct and little can be done to save them.

    Ⓑ Big cats are unique creatures that deserve our respect.

    Ⓒ Many cats are dangerous to humans and should be left alone.

    Ⓓ Lions and tigers have very different needs.

9. Which statement is true?

    Ⓐ The poem is meant to entertain, while the article is meant to inform the reader.

    Ⓑ Both the poem and the article are meant to inform the reader.

    Ⓒ The poem is meant to inform, while the article is meant to entertain the reader.

    Ⓓ Both the poem and the article are meant to entertain the reader.

Name: _____ Date: _____

A Holiday on Ice

Directions: Read this text and answer the questions on page 95.

1   Santiago was tired of the ice, ice, and more ice—that's all he could see in every direction. It shone and sparkled in the harsh light, but it wasn't flat like the ice at a skating rink or a frozen pond. This ice was crazy. Huge slabs stood up at weird angles; large chunks of ice lay piled in heaps. The ice under his skis was cracked and broken, and large holes appeared out of nowhere as the group struggled along.

2   The worst part was the areas where there was no ice. The group of skiers kept running into leads—jagged cracks where there was nothing but open water. Most of the time, the leads were too big to ski or jump across, which meant they had to turn left or right and go far out of their way until they found solid ice again. They certainly didn't want to fall into the dangerously cold Arctic water.

3   Santiago glanced over his shoulder at his wife, Janice. She was right behind him, skiing along and smiling. He noticed that she wasn't even breathing hard. "Tell me again why we're doing this," he panted.

The tough, icy Arctic

Tortle/Corbis Sygma

A Holiday on Ice *(cont.)*

4   "Are you kidding?" she replied. "Skiing to the North Pole is the greatest adventure we've ever been on! We'll remember this for the rest of our lives!"

5   "Oh, yeah," Santiago grumbled. Well, it had seemed like an exciting idea when Janice first planned the trip, he thought. They should have flown all the way to the Pole, but instead they had signed up to ski the last few miles. Now, Santiago's muscles burned, and his lungs ached from breathing the freezing cold air.

6   Just then, Jared, their guide, shouted from the front of the line, "Okay, we made it! We're here!"

7   There were whoops and hollers from the members of the group as they gathered around Jared. Everyone started snapping photos.

8   "What?" Santiago blurted out. "This is it? This is the North Pole?"

9   "This is it," Jared confirmed. "Good work, everyone!"

10 "What were you expecting?" Janice asked with one eyebrow raised. "A big red-and-white pole?"

11 "I don't know," Santiago answered, rubbing the back of his head and looking all around. "I just thought there'd be something besides ice."

The North Pole

A Holiday on Ice (cont.)

Directions: Fill in the bubble of each correct answer choice.

1. Which statement from the text shows Santiago's feelings about the trip? There is more than one correct answer.

   Ⓐ "Skiing to the North Pole is the greatest adventure we've ever been on!"

   Ⓑ "There were whoops and hollers from the members of the group as they gathered around Jared."

   Ⓒ "I just thought there'd be something besides ice."

   Ⓓ "They should have flown all the way to the Pole, but instead they had signed up to ski the last few miles."

2. Why did the author include the first photograph with the story?

   Ⓐ to show the direction the characters are traveling

   Ⓑ to show the harsh setting for the story

   Ⓒ to show the equipment the characters are carrying

   Ⓓ to prove there is no red-and-white pole at the North Pole

3. Which sentence uses the word *leads* in the same way as it used in paragraph 2?

   Ⓐ The hikers could no longer continue due to the dangerous leads on the path.

   Ⓑ The guide leads the group across the dangerous ice to safety.

   Ⓒ Janice leads the race by over two hundred yards.

   Ⓓ The trail of ice leads to the North Pole.

Name: _____   Date: _____

On Top of the World

Directions: Read this text and answer the questions on page 98.

1   It happened more than 60 years ago. On May 29, 1953, Edmund Hillary and Tenzing Norgay stood on top of the world. They were the first people to reach the top of Mount Everest. It is the world's tallest mountain. Mount Everest stands in the middle of Asia. It is on the borders of Nepal and China. The mountain stands 29,035 feet (8,848 meters) above sea level. More than 100 years went by from the time scientists discovered that the mountain was the world's tallest to when Hillary and Norgay climbed it. During those years, many people wanted to be the first to the top. Now, the two men had done it. But as they stood on the snow-covered peak, they didn't have time to celebrate.

Royal Geographical Society

Norgay and Hillary on Everest

2   Hillary stated about the moment at the top, "I didn't leap or throw my hands in the air. We were tired, of course." They had to hurry back down the mountain. They needed to get back to camp before dark.

A Lasting Friendship

3   More than 200 men and women have died trying to climb Everest. There are many dangers: ice, snow, wind, and little oxygen. Then there are huge, deep cracks called crevasses, through which a climber can fall. "You cannot conquer Everest," says Jamling Norgay. He is Tenzing's son. "Everest will give you a chance to stand on top. That's it."

4   After Everest, both Hillary and Norgay became famous all over the world. Hillary led other expeditions. One went to the South Pole. Norgay became an official for a group that studied mountain climbing. The two men stayed good friends.

On Top of the World (cont.)

5   Norgay died in 1986. But Hillary and his son, Peter, remained good friends with Jamling. Jamling and Peter climbed Everest together.

6   The friendship between the two families meant much more than climbing. Together they worked to make conditions better for Norgay's people, the Sherpas. The Sherpas are a group of people who live in Nepal. Many work as guides for mountain climbers.

7   Sir Edmund Hillary died in 2008. He had worked to bring schools and hospitals to Sherpa towns. "That's how I'd like to be remembered," he said. "Not for Everest, but for the work I did with my Sherpa friends." When he thought of those friendships, he still felt as though he were on top of the world.

Royal Geographical Society

Sherpas carry supplies on Everest.

Name: _____   Date: _____

On Top of the World (cont.)

Directions: Fill in the bubble of each correct answer choice.

4. What detail from the text helps explain the idea behind the title for this story?

   Ⓐ "It happened more than 60 years ago."

   Ⓑ "Now, the two men had done it."

   Ⓒ "After Everest, both Hillary and Norgay became famous all over the world."

   Ⓓ "Not for Everest, but for the work I did with my Sherpa friends."

5. Read this sentence from paragraph 3: "'You cannot conquer Everest,' says Jamling Norgay." Which sentence from the article explains the meaning of his statement?

   Ⓐ "More than 100 years went by from the time scientists discovered that the mountain was the world's tallest to when Hillary and Norgay climbed it."

   Ⓑ "Everest will give you a chance to stand on top. That's it."

   Ⓒ "It is the world's tallest mountain."

   Ⓓ "The mountain stands 29,035 feet (8,848 meters) above sea level."

6. Which other sentence from the text supports the answer to number 5?

   Ⓔ "During those years, many people wanted to be the first to the top."

   Ⓕ "There are many dangers: ice, snow, wind, and little oxygen."

   Ⓖ "The two men stayed good friends."

   Ⓗ "Norgay became an official for a group that studied mountain climbing."

© Shell Education

Name: _____ Date: _____

A Holiday on Ice and On Top of the World

Directions: Reread the texts on pages 93–94 and 96–97. Then, fill in the bubble of each correct answer choice.

---

7. Both the story and the article are similar in that . . .

    Ⓐ the people accomplish a major feat.

    Ⓑ they are set in the same area of the world.

    Ⓒ an unexpected twist takes place to change the reader's viewpoint.

    Ⓓ a catastrophe occurs at the end.

---

8. Which feature from both the article and the story best helps the reader visualize the conditions and the surroundings the people experienced?

    Ⓐ the titles

    Ⓑ bolded words

    Ⓒ the captions

    Ⓓ the photographs

---

9. Which word best describes both Janice from the story and Edmund Hillary from the article?

    Ⓐ intelligent

    Ⓑ determined

    Ⓒ out-spoken

    Ⓓ attentive

References Cited

Conley, David T. 2014. "Common Core Development and Substance." *Social Policy Report* 28 (2): 1–15.

Kornhaber, Mindy L., Kelly Griffith, and Alison Tyler. 2014. "It's Not Education by Zip Code Anymore—But What is It? Conceptions of Equity under the Common Core." *Education Policy Analysis Archives* 22 (4): 1–26. doi:10.14507/epaa.v22n4.2014.

National Governors Association Center for Best Practices, Council of Chief State School Officers. 2010. *Common Core State Standards*. National Governors Association Center for Best Practices, Council of Chief State School Officers: Washington D.C. http://www.corestandards.org/about-the-standards/frequently-asked-questions/.

Partnership for Assessment of Readiness for College and Careers. 2013. *The PARCC Assessment.* PARCC: Washington, D.C. http://www.parcconline.org/about-parcc.

Rothman, Robert. 2013. *Common Core State Standards 101*. http://all4ed.org/reports-factsheets/common-core-state-standards-101/.

Texas Education Agency. 2014. *State of Texas Assessment of Academic Readiness: A Parent's Guide to the Student Testing Program.* TEA: Texas.

The Smarter Balanced Assessment Consortium. 2014. *Smarter Balanced Assessment Consortium.* California Department of Education. http://www.smarterbalanced.org/about/member-states/.

Wiley, Terrence G., and Wayne E. Wright. 2004. "Against the Undertow: Language-Minority Education Policy and Politics in the 'Age of Accountability.'" *Educational Policy*, 18 (1): 142–168. doi:10.1177/0895904803260030.

Question Types

The following chart correlates each question in this book to one of the three categories of questions. For more information on the categories of questions, see pages 7–9.

Practice Exercise Title	Item	Key Ideas and Details	Craft and Structure	Integration of Knowledge and Ideas
Before He Changed the World (pages 13–16)	1		x	
	2	x		
	3	x		
	4		x	
	5	x		
	6			x
	7	x		
	8	x		
Little Bugs, Big Stink (pages 17–20)	1		x	
	2	x		
	3		x	
	4	x		
	5	x		
	6			x
	7	x		
	8	x		
Lighting the Way (pages 21–24)	1	x		
	2			x
	3		x	
	4		x	
	5	x		
	6	x		
	7	x		
	8		x	
Hoop Dreams (pages 25–28)	1	x		
	2			x
	3		x	
	4	x		
	5	x		
	6		x	
	7	x		
	8		x	
They're Back! (pages 29–32)	1	x		
	2		x	
	3		x	
	4			x
	5	x		
	6	x		
	7	x		
	8	x		

Question Types *(cont.)*

Practice Exercise Title	Item	Key Ideas and Details	Craft and Structure	Integration of Knowledge and Ideas
How Great Is Harry Potter? (pages 33–37)	1		x	
	2		x	
	3	x		
	4			x
	5	x		
	6	x		
	7	x		
	8		x	
The Iditarod Is the Best Sport in the World (pages 38–42)	1		x	
	2		x	
	3			x
	4	x		
	5	x		
	6	x		
	7		x	
	8	x		
Johann Gutenberg and the Printing Press (pages 43–47)	1		x	
	2		x	
	3	x		
	4			x
	5	x		
	6	x		
	7	x		
	8			x
Anansi's Sons (pages 48–51)	1			x
	2		x	
	3	x		
	4		x	
	5	x		
	6	x		
	7	x		
	8			x
Bread and Roses (pages 52–56)	1	x		
	2		x	
	3		x	
	4			x
	5	x		
	6	x		
	7		x	
	8	x		

Question Types *(cont.)*

Practice Exercise Title	Item	Key Ideas and Details	Craft and Structure	Integration of Knowledge and Ideas
The Cause of the Mutiny (pages 57–61)	1	x		
	2		x	
	3	x		
	4		x	
	5	x		
	6			x
	7	x		
	8		x	
Mr. Nobody (pages 62–65)	1	x		
	2	x		
	3	x		
	4		x	
	5		x	
	6			x
	7	x		
	8	x		
The Sun's Travels (pages 66–69)	1	x		
	2		x	
	3	x		
	4		x	
	5	x		
	6			x
	7	x		
Two Flat Friends Travel the World (pages 70–75)	1		x	
	2	x		
	3			x
	4		x	
	5	x		
	6			x
	7	x		
	8	x		
Life in a Continental Camp (pages 76–81)	1	x		
	2	x		
	3	x		
	4			x
	5		x	
	6		x	
	7	x		
	8	x		

Question Types *(cont.)*

Practice Exercise Title	Item	Key Ideas and Details	Craft and Structure	Integration of Knowledge and Ideas
John Henry (pages 82–87)	1	x		
	2		x	
	3			x
	4	x		
	5	x		
	6		x	
	7	x		
	8	x		
The Lion (pages 88–89)	1	x		
	2	x		
	3		x	
A Big Home for Big Cats (pages 90–91)	4			x
	5	x		
	6		x	
The Lion and A Big Home for Big Cats (page 92)	7			x
	8			x
	9			x
A Holiday on Ice (pages 93–95)	1	x		
	2			x
	3		x	
On Top of the World (pages 96–98)	4		x	
	5	x		
	6	x		
A Holiday on Ice and On Top of the World (page 99)	7			x
	8			x
	9			x

   © Shell Education

Testing Tips

Reading

READ more nonfiction texts with students!

Writing

Encourage students to **SHOW** what they know with text-based **PROOF**!

How Do I Help Students Prepare for Today's Tests?

Mathematics

Help students **EXPLAIN** what's in their brains and **CONNECT** mathematics to the real world!

Listening

DISCUSS what you read! **ANALYZE** what you think! **SYNTHESIZE** information!!

Testing Tips *(cont.)*

Jail the Detail!		Highlight, underline, or circle the details in the questions. This helps FOCUS on what the question is asking.
Be Slick and Predict!		Predict what the answer is BEFORE you read the choices!
Slash the Trash!		Read ALL the answer choices. "Trash" the choices that you know are incorrect.
Plug It In! Plug It In!		Once you choose an answer, PLUG IT IN! Make sure your answer makes sense, especially with vocabulary and math.
Be Smart with Charts! Zap the Maps!		Charts and maps provide information that you can use to answer some questions. Analyze ALL information before answering a question!
Extra! Extra! Read All About It!		If the directions say read . . . READ! Pay close attention to signal words in the directions, such as *explain*, *interpret*, and *compare*.
If You Snooze, You Might Lose!		Do not leave questions unanswered. Answering questions increases your chances of getting correct answers!
Check It Out!		After you complete the test, go back and check your work!

Answer Key

Before He Changed the World (pages 13–16)

1. B. to show that Martin made a difference in the lives of many people
2. H. "It was the first of many protests Martin would lead."
3. A. Martin was a regular kid.
4. C. to protect someone or something
5. D. Martin's life before he became famous.
6. C. It provides a glimpse of Martin as a boy.
7. Martin's white friends tell him that they can no longer play with him. He feels this is wrong and decides he's going to change things by "turning the world upside down."
8. Age 7—Martin's white friends stop playing with him; Age 15—Martin goes to college; Age 25—Martin becomes a pastor; Age 26—Martin leads a bus boycott.

Little Bugs, Big Stink (pages 17–20)

1. D. scientist
2. D. October
3. B. The stinkbugs are unwelcome guests.
4. C. Scientists are not sure why the stinkbug population is increasing.
5. E. "Nobody really knows why there were so many that year."
6. A. "Stinkbugs cause trouble in the environment."
7. Scientists plan on creating a chemical to help trap stinkbugs or using the stinkbug's natural enemies to eliminate it.
8. Accept any two of these statements:
   • "They eat fruit and vegetable crops."
   • "They have caused millions of dollars in crop losses for American farmers."
   • "American farmers hope scientists solve this stinky problem soon!"

Lighting the Way (pages 21–24)

1. C. She wants to help people in places that lack electricity.
2. A. "What inspired this idea?"
   D. "How does it feel to compete in the science fair?"
3. B. "The tiles draw heat from your hand and also from the surrounding air."
4. D. continue creating inventions.
5. E. She wants to finish the flashlight's design.
   G. She hopes her flashlight will help people in poor countries.
   H. She is working on a hands-free headlamp for kids.
6. C. creates a solution to a problem in another part of the world.
7. The answer should be numbered this way:
   • 4—Ann enters the flashlight in the 2013 Google Science Fair.
   • 1—Poor families do not have enough money to pay for electricity.
   • 3—Ann decides to create a flashlight that would not need batteries.
   • 2—Students have a difficult time completing their homework.
8. Most people in the United States or Canada have electricity. Therefore, studying or working at night is not a problem. Ann invented her flashlight in order to help people in places without reliable electric power.

Hoop Dreams (pages 25–28)

1. C. to keep a tradition going
2. B. R.J. is putting on a show for an audience.
3. D. He is confident.
4. D. "People clapped when he held hoops together to look like an eagle's wings."
5. G. telling a story about turtles using hoops
6. A. to show that the traditions of the family are important
7. R.J. begins with five hoops. He picks up more hoops. He spins them on his arms. He jumps through hoops. Finally, he holds the hoops together to form an eagle's wings while dancing.
8. R.J. learns the dances by copying his uncles. This shows that family is an important part of R.J.'s hoop dancing.

Answer Key *(cont.)*

They're Back! (pages 29–32)

1. B. a Tyrannosaurus rex
2. C. living things that have been eliminated from the planet
3. E. clearing a forest to build a new town
4. C. Scientists are considering bringing them back.
5. A. "In 2003, a team of Spanish and French scientists re-created the Pyrenean ibex."
6. B. People are responsible for the extinction of many animals.
7. Students should underline this text:
   - "Or might they crowd out existing species?"
   - "And will people work less hard to protect animals if they know that scientists can reverse our mistakes?"
8. Accept any two quotations:
   - "Researchers need DNA to bring back a species."
   - "Dinosaurs have been gone for too long."
   - "None of their DNA remains in fossils."

How Great Is Harry Potter? (pages 33–37)

1. B. The author believes the Harry Potter books are great but have some flaws.
2. G. "Though the books are far from perfect, on the whole, they are great literature."
3. A. Harry Potter is a great character.
4. B. "They've been printed in 73 languages."
   D. "As of 2013, more than 450 million copies of the Harry Potter books had been sold."
5. C. the language
6. C. flying cars
   D. flavored candies
7. The chart might include the following examples:

Harry Potter—Far From Perfect!
   - "The characters aren't complex."
   - "Probably the greatest weakness of the books is the lack of descriptive language."
   - "Rowling's gift for inventing places, characters, and plots is not matched by her ability to describe them."

Harry Potter—Great Literature!
   - "Author J. K. Rowling has created an original, amazing world."
   - "Rowling's imagination has also produced many memorable characters."
   - "Things move quickly."
   - "There's lots of action."
   - "What makes Rowling's books true classics, however, is Harry Potter himself."
   - "Rowling makes the world of Hogwarts real and thrilling."
8. Students can defend either side of this issue. However, they need to provide evidence from their graphic organizer or directly from the text to support their opinions.

The Iditarod Is the Best Sport in the World (pages 38–42)

1. D. to convince the reader that the Iditarod dog-sled race is the greatest sport
2. E. " . . . sled dogs run 42.3 times farther than marathon runners."
   G. "Go check out some real athletes and a real sport."
3. B. Sled dogs are amazing athletes.
   D. The Iditarod takes place once a year.
4. C. "The race follows the 1925 route of a dog team."
5. A. They keep the dogs warm.
6. D. The dogs must work together and not bite each other.
7. The following information was shared about the four sports:
   - football—It's only exciting when a player does a dance after a touchdown.
   - baseball—Games sometimes feel like they are 10 days long.
   - marathon—Runners only run for a "measly" 26.2 miles (42.2 km).
   - hockey—It is played on indoor ice.
8. Main idea: The Iditarod is the best sport in the world, and it has the world's greatest athletes. Supporting details may vary but can include: Sled dogs have endurance, speed, stamina, strength, and determination. It is a tradition that has taken place since 1925.

Answer Key *(cont.)*

Johann Gutenberg and the Printing Press
(pages 43–47)

1. A. meaning 1

2. F. "set the letters into"

3. A. Most people could not read or write.

   B. There were no newspapers or magazines.

4. C. to give the reader a sense of what it looked like

5. D. "His final design worked so well that it remained the same for nearly 400 years."

6. A. the history of printing

7. The answers should be numbered as follows:
   - 2—Arrange the type in a frame.
   - 5—Press paper against the type.
   - 1—Create the metal letters, or type.
   - 3—Place the frame in the press.
   - 4—Apply ink to the type.
   - 6—Allow the page to dry.

8. The Venn diagram may include the following responses:
   - Japan and China circle—used carved wooden blocks around the year 700 C.E.
   - Korea circle—invented metal type years after other Asian nations
   - Intersection of circles—created ways to print prior to Germany

Anansi's Sons (pages 48–51)

1. D. It helps the reader to visualize the danger that Anansi is in.

2. A. It provides background information about Anansi.

3. A. They all have unique talents.
   D. They have names that tell what they can do.

4. B. "He fell but fortunately Cushion waited on the ground to give his father a soft, safe landing."

5. H. "Finally, Anansi was free from danger."

6. C. the moon

7. The sons should be listed with short descriptions:
   - See Trouble—realizes that Anansi is in trouble
   - Road Builder—carves a path through the woods
   - River Drinker—drinks up the river
   - Game Skinner—cuts open the fish to free Anansi
   - Stone Thrower—throws a rock at the bird
   - Cushion—provides a soft spot to land

8. Students should choose a son and describe, using textual evidence, why that son is the most helpful.

Bread and Roses (pages 52–56)

1. B. providing safer work conditions and earning more money

2. D. machines

3. F. They are very noisy.

4. B. barefoot workers

5. C. "Instead we all have to work just to make ends meet."

6. A. He does not attend school in America.

7. The Venn diagram may include the following responses:
   - Salvatore circle—age 10, been working longer, from Italy, learning to read English
   - Jedrek circle—age 11, worried about the foreman, can read English
   - Intersection of circles—textile workers, young boys, helping family, want better conditions and more pay

8. Jedrek is an 11-year-old boy at the factory. In the story, he worries about the foreman and is the one who can already read English. Salvatore is 10 years old. He has been working longer than Jedrek. He was born in Italy and is learning to read English. Both boys work in the factory. They are trying to help their families by working. Both Jedrek and Salvatore would like better working conditions and pay.

Answer Key (cont.)

The Cause of the Mutiny (pages 57–61)

1. B. "But just then, the captain turned to leave Lord John and Lady Alice."

2. C. to describe the captain's reaction to being embarrassed

3. E. "He overturned the water pail, too, and was drenched in its dirty contents."

   G. "The captain sprawled face first upon the deck."

4. D. "With a snarl, he sprang upon the captain and crushed him to his knees with one mighty blow."

5. B. "He did not dare to anger an English official.

   D. "The queen's mighty arm wielded an instrument which he feared—England's navy."

6. A. the captain's response to the sailors' behavior

7. The captain is a very strict leader. He angers very easily when he feels he is disrespected. Some examples from the text include:

   • "His face darkened with the scarlet of rage."

   • "With a terrific blow, he knocked the sailor to the deck."

   • "He fired point blank at the great mountain of muscle towering before him."

8. Personality traits for Lord John Greystoke include: thoughtful, peaceful, disgusted with the captain, quick thinking. Text support for this list includes the following:

   • "But, quick as he was, John was almost as quick."

   • "Lord Greystoke had struck down the captain's arm when he saw the gun flash in the sun."

   • "John made it plain that he was disgusted with the brutality displayed toward the crew."

   • "He would not tolerate anything further of the kind while he and Lady Greystoke were passengers."

Mr. Nobody (pages 62–65)

1. D. "Who does the mischief that is done in everybody's house!"

2. B. "The fingerprints upon the door by none of us are made."

3. B. line 3

4. D. hearing

5. G. "I know a funny little man who's as quiet as a mouse"

6. A. There is a rhyming pattern in the poem.

   D. Each stanza consists of four lines.

7. Accept any three of these examples: Mr. Nobody is like a young child because he drops plates and breaks them, spills milk, tears buttons off of shirts, leaves fingerprints on the door, tears pages in a book, and leaves his boots lying around.

8. The graphic organizer can include some of the following answers:

   • Destroys items: broken plates, torn books, buttons off shirts

   • Forgets to do things: leaves the door ajar, leaves the blinds open

   • Makes a mess: fingerprints on door, spilled milk, boots lying around

The Sun's Travels (pages 66–69)

1. C. "At night upon my pillow lie."

2. B. Somewhere it is always the opposite time of day from where the author is.

3. E. lines 1 and 2

4. A. line 3

5. D. "And all the children in the West"

6. C. Some of the lines are incomplete sentences.

7. Students' answers will vary, but may include similarities such as: Each of the poems alludes to the Earth's orbit and its effect on day or night; Each poem mentions lying in bed. Differences may include: The last stanza of "The Moon's Travels" mentions East rather than West. "The Sun's Travels" is written by a famous poet and "The Moon's Travels" is written by a fourth grader.

Answer Key *(cont.)*

Two Flat Friends Travel the World
(pages 70–75)

1. B. present historical facts in an entertaining way.
2. C. "They believed the gold and treasures would be needed during the afterlife."

   D. "I also took them to see the Nile, the longest river in the world."
3. A. They both present facts.
4. C. Mazu presents historical facts to the reader.
5. F. "Did you know that the ancient Chinese carried their emperors on litters?"
6. C. A ruler used life-size clay soldiers to protect him after death.
7.

Item	Egypt	China
pharaohs	x	
Terra-cotta Warriors		x
pyramids	x	
emperors		x
sphinx	x	
Nile	x	
Great Wall		x
hieroglyphics	x	
mummies	x	
Forbidden City		x

8. Students should choose one country and use textual evidence to describe various aspects of life.

Life in a Continental Camp (pages 76–81)

1. A. "General Lafayette, will you lead the attack?"
2. G. "But, sir, no amount of spirit will make up for the lack of soldiers!"
3. D. "Molly! The young man was just stating his opinion."
4. D. The narrator explains things that would be hard to include as conversation.
5. C. "As each egg falls into her right hand, she cracks it before it lands perfectly in the hot frying pan."
6. B. a side of a military formation
7. The Venn diagram may include the following responses:
   - Molly "Pitcher" Hays circle—has a temper; works as a cook and seamstress; married to William
   - George Washington circle—calm; is the General of the army; believes in his army's power
   - Intersection of circles—opinionated; good leader
8. Students should choose one character to describe, using textual evidence, about how he or she plays an important role at the Continental Army camp.

John Henry (pages 82–87)

1. C. "he was so strong"
2. A. Ma
3. D. dialogue
4. B. He is larger and stronger than most men.
5. E. " . . . that mountain blocked the sun!"
6. C. a sudden, hard strike
7. The answers are as follows:
   - Polly Ann—"This story begins on the day of jubilation . . . ."
   - Boss—"Well, you've come to the right place."
   - Worker 2—"That's unbelievable!"
   - John Henry—"This hammer feels just right in my hand."
   - Worker 1—"I couldn't help but stare, for he was something to behold!"
   - Ma—"They worked him hard—yes, they did."
8. Details from the text will vary, but may include:
   - It took the other workers multiple blows of a hammer when it only took John Henry one.
   - He had brawn.
   - He could wield a hammer "As well as any man could."

Answer Key *(cont.)*

The Lion (pages 88–89)

1. B. the sound a lion makes
2. G. "Know his terror-breathing call."
3. D. line 11

A Big Home for Big Cats (pages 90–91)

4. D. India
5. A. "And if a big cat gets canine distemper, it is a death sentence."
6. B. meaning 2

The Lion and A Big Home for Big Cats (page 92)

7. C. The article mentions different big cats, while the poem focuses on one.
8. B. Big cats are unique creatures that deserve our respect.
9. A. The poem is meant to entertain, while the article is meant to inform the reader.

A Holiday on Ice (pages 93–95)

1. C. "I just thought there'd be something besides ice."

   D. "They should have flown all the way to the Pole, but instead they had signed up to ski the last few miles."
2. B. to show the harsh setting for the story
3. A. The hikers could no longer continue due to the dangerous leads on the path.

On Top of the World (pages 96–98)

4. D. "Not for Everest, but for the work I did with my Sherpa friends."
5. B. "Everest will give you a chance to stand on top. That's it."
6. F. "There are many dangers: ice, snow, wind, and little oxygen."

A Holiday on Ice and On Top of the World (page 99)

7. A. the people accomplish a major feat.
8. D. the photographs
9. B. determined

© *Shell Education*